# WHO WAS EDGAR CAYCE?

**EDGAR CAYCE,** unwitting seer and clairvoyant, touched millions of lives with his innate spiritual wisdom and his uncanny healing visions.

Born in 1877 in Hopkinsville, Kentucky, Edgar Cayce had a seventh-grade education, yet was able to repeat complex and technical medical jargon when under a trance. In this state, he was said to heal many of the people who came seeking his counsel with his recommendations for medical treatment. Cayce soon began to talk about spiritual notions such as Atlantis, reincarnation, dreams, astrology, and more. He would also predict some of the more astounding events of the twentieth century, such as World Wars and the Great Depression.

*The Washington Post* wrote: "His words have inspired faith in spirituality, which for many people is more powerful than science." Called the "sleeping prophet" and "America's greatest psychic," Cayce, who died in 1945, may have been the first to usher in what is now known as the New Age Movement. More than fifty years after his death, his work continues to influence our lives in powerful new ways.

## Books in the Edgar Cayce series from St. Martin's Paperbacks

# AWAKENING YOUR PSYCHIC POWERS

## HENRY REED

WITH A FOREWORD BY CHARLES THOMAS CAYCE

St. Martin's Paperbacks

AWAKENING YOUR PSYCHIC POWERS

Copyright © 1988 by Henry Reed.

"Who Was Edgar Cayce?" copyright © 1995 by William A. McGarey, M.D.

"The Healing Work of Edgar Cayce Continues" copyright © 1996 by Mark Thurston, Ph.D.

Cover photograph by Photonica.

For information address St. Martin's Press, 175 Fifth Avenue, New York, NY 10010.

Library of Congress Catalog Card Number: 87-46223

ISBN: 0-312-95868-4
EAN: 80312-95868-8

Printed in the United States of America

Harper & Row trade paperback edition published 1988
St. Martin's Paperbacks edition / June 1996

St. Martin's Paperbacks are published by St. Martin's Press, 175 Fifth Avenue, New York, NY 10010.

20   19   18   17   16   15   14   13   12

# CONTENTS

## PART IV: DEVELOPING PSYCHIC AWARENESS   199

# FOREWORD

IT IS A TIME in the earth when people everywhere
seek to know more of the mysteries of the mind, the
soul," said my grandfather, Edgar Cayce, from an unconscious trance from which he demonstrated a remarkable gift for clairvoyance.

His words are prophetic even today, as more and
more Americans in these unsettled times are turning to
psychic explanations for daily events. For example, according to a national survey by the National Opinion
Research Council nearly half of American adults today
believe they have been in contact with someone who has
died, a figure twice that of ten years ago. Two-thirds of
all adults say they have had an ESP experience; ten
years ago that figure was only one-half.

Every culture throughout history has made note of its
own members' gifted powers beyond the five senses.
These rare individuals held special interest because they
seemed able to provide solutions to life's pressing problems. America in the twentieth century is no exception.

Edgar Cayce was perhaps the most famous and most
carefully documented psychic of our time. He began to
use his unusual abilities when he was a young man, and
from then on for over forty years he would, usually twice
a day, lie on a couch, go into a sleeplike state, and respond to questions. Over fourteen thousand of these
discourses, called readings, were carefully transcribed
by his secretary and preserved by the Edgar Cayce
Foundation in Virginia Beach, Virginia. These psychic
readings continue to provide inspiration, insight, and
help with healing to tens of thousands of people.

Having only an eighth-grade education, Edgar Cayce
lived a plain and simple life by the world's standards. As
early as his childhood in Hopkinsville, Kentucky, however, he sensed that he had psychic ability. While alone

one day he had a vision of a woman who told him he would have unusual power to help people. He also related experiences of "seeing" dead relatives. Once, while struggling with school lessons, he slept on his spelling book and awakened knowing the entire contents of the book.

As a young man he experimented with hypnosis to treat a recurring throat problem that caused him to lose his speech. He discovered that under hypnosis he could diagnose and describe treatments for the physical ailments of others, often without knowing or seeing the person with the ailment. People began to ask him other sorts of questions, and he found himself able to answer these as well.

In 1910 the *New York Times* published a two-page story with pictures about Edgar Cayce's psychic ability as described by a young physician, Wesley Ketchum, to a clinical research society in Boston. From that time on people from all over the country with every conceivable question sought his help.

In addition to his unusual talents, Cayce was a deeply religious man who taught Sunday school all of his adult life and read the entire Bible once for every year that he lived. He always tried to attune himself to God's will by studying the Scriptures and maintaining a rich prayer life, as well as by trying to be of service to those who came seeking help. He used his talents only for helpful purposes. Cayce's simplicity and humility and his commitment to doing good in the world continue to attract people to the story of his life and work and to the far-reaching information he gave.

In this series we hope to provide the reader with insights in the search for understanding and meaning in life. Each book in the series explores its subject from the viewpoint of the Edgar Cayce readings and compares the perspectives of other metaphysical literature and of current scientific thought. The interested reader needs no prior knowledge of the Cayce information. When one of the Edgar Cayce readings is quoted, the identifying number of that reading is included for those who may wish to read the full text. Each volume includes suggestions for further study.

This book, *Awakening Your Psychic Powers* by Henry Reed, Ph.D., elaborates on a theme Edgar Cayce often mentioned, that each of us has psychic ability that we can learn to use profitably. Dr. Reed, formerly a member of the staff of the Association for Research and Enlightenment, is highly qualified to write on this subject. Formerly a teacher at Princeton University, Dr. Reed is a lecturer, writer, licensed psychologist with a private practice, and a professor at Atlantic University. I feel confident you will find his comprehensive approach an awakening experience.

*Charles Thomas Cayce, Ph.D.*
*President*
*Association for Research and Enlightenment*

# PREFACE

THE PSYCHIC IS *REAL*. This book invites you to awaken your psychic awareness, and provides a perspective from which it can develop.

I have based this book on the insights Edgar Cayce received in psychic trance, and the way he incorporated those insights into his daily life. Cayce would not ask you to take these ideas on faith. He would ask you to test the validity of this material in your own life, use what proves constructive, and discard the rest.

As a former university professor, I am accustomed to discussing theory before dealing with practice. Part I is therefore devoted to exploring some universal concepts that serve to explain the nature of reality, and how psychic awareness is a natural part of that reality. Part II discusses some of the more common psychic experiences and how to evoke them—through intuition, dreams, meditation, and hypnosis. Part III probes the role of the body, mind, and soul in psychic awareness. Finally, Part IV presents some experiments for you to try in your adventure into this exciting realm, and discusses the ultimate purpose of psychic awareness.

As I wrote this book, I kept hearing these words repeated in the back of my mind: "See it, feel it, touch it, taste it, smell it, believe it, live it." If this book helps you become so aware of the psychic that you can make it real in your life, then its mission has been accomplished.

In this effort, I have to thank those people whose earlier efforts explaining the meaning and significance of Edgar Cayce's trance readings made this book possible: Harmon Bro, Hugh Lynn Cayce, Everett Irion, Herbert Puryear, and Mark Thurston. I also appreciate the untiring editorial efforts of A. Robert Smith, who has cared very much that this book be easy for you to read. And for making sure that all the examples and explanations are worth reading, I have to thank my wife, Veronica Lyn.

A long line of people, reaching at least as far back as Pythagoras and moving up through the names above, are very interested in your becoming psychic. The psychic has been real to them and they've helped me try to make it real for you.

# Part I

# THE PSYCHIC IMAGINATION

# 1

# IMAGINE BEING PSYCHIC

*The study from the human standpoint, of
subconscious, subliminal, psychic, soul forces, is
and should be the great study for the human
family, for through self man will understand its
Maker when it understands its relation to its
Maker, and it will only understand that through
itself, and that understanding is the knowledge as
is given here in this state.*

EDGAR CAYCE reading no. 3744–4*

*People who go into this without spiritual
aspirations should be warned that unless they
remain open-minded about the possibility of being
led into deeper meanings of life, their experience
will almost certainly turn out to be a blind alley.
For people who covet psychic potency out of profit
and power, my advice is unequivocal: either
develop higher motivation or drop the whole
business at once. The consequences of deliberate
misuse of these abilities can be disastrous.*

ARTHUR FORD

* Each of the Edgar Cayce readings has been assigned a two-part number to provide easy reference. Each person who received a reading was given an anonymous number; this is the first half of the two-part number. Since many individuals obtained more than one reading, the second number designates the number of that reading in the series. Reading no. 3744–4 was given for a person who was assigned case number 3744. This particular reading was the fourth one that person obtained from Cayce.

WHEN I LIE ON my back on a warm summer's night and gaze up at the spectacle of the stars, my mind naturally floats upward into the enormity of the universe and I seem to merge with the stars. This earthen platform of our planet, usually such a solid foundation, becomes an ever-shrinking, wobbly pebble in the huge, glittering blackness of space. My imagination, and I with it, expand into the infinite. I am engulfed in a tingling chill. Overwhelmed, I suddenly snap back to solid earth. But, I ask myself, what happened? Was what I sensed really true? Was it really possible that my mind could rise and join the stars in heaven?

As I ponder this mystery, I know I am not alone. The Native Americans, for example, have a tradition that they came from the stars and to the stars they will return. What enshrouded secret of their sacred imagination links them with the stars? Another traveler, the English "imagineer" Olaf Stapleton, shared his psychic journey into space with us in his book *Star Maker*. His mind encountered not only other worlds, but was able to commune with other minds, travelers all in a multidimensional universal consciousness. In an attempt to keep us grounded on earth, he called his account "science fiction." Nevertheless, in the guise of such fiction, the imagination is the first pioneer; science and technology then follow, building concrete steps for all to climb. The imagination is an unbounded traveler, often returning with surprising souvenirs to lure successive generations of adventurers. To the stars we once visited only in our dreams and in our imagination, we now sent rockets and spacecraft.

## A PSYCHIC PROBE OF OUTER SPACE

In December 1973 *Pioneer 10*'s observations about the planet Jupiter began to reach NASA scientists, who were millions of miles away on earth. Some of its observations contradicted astronomers' long-held assumptions about this revered planet. *Pioneer 10*'s discoveries came as no surprise, however, to two men who had "seen" Jupiter nine months earlier.

In an experiment organized by the Stanford Research Institute, two gifted psychics, Ingo Swann and Harold Sherman, traveled psychically to Jupiter while scientists recorded their impressions. Swann was in California, Sherman in Arkansas. Their impressions were amazingly similar to each other, and opposed to scientific speculation: both visualized a deadly radiation ring around Jupiter and an upper atmosphere of colorful frozen crystals; they said that the planet itself was very warm, but was whipped by violent windstorms. *Pioneer 10*'s data later contradicted the scientists' speculation, and confirmed the amazing accuracy of the atmospheric observations of Swann and Sherman, our first psychic astronauts.

About a year later, they repeated their feat on a "visit" to Mercury. Again, they gave similar reports on what they had seen. Moreover, when the data from NASA's *Mariner 10* space probe began to reach earth from Mercury, it contradicted conventional scientific speculation and confirmed the psychics' observations. Scientists had assumed that Mercury was too hot to support an atmosphere and that it revolved too slowly to have a magnetic field. But the two psychics sensed a thin atmosphere, as well as a magnetic field. Another astounding correspondence between the reports of the psychics and the data from *Mariner 10* was the discovery of a helium "tail" coming out of Mercury and heading away from the sun. In *To Kiss Earth Goodbye,* Swann describes the excitement he felt when newspapers printed descriptions of Mercury that were much like his own psychic impressions.

Can you imagine traveling psychically to another planet? How do you imagine that these two psychics made the trip? Words like "travel," of course, suggest physical movement. Swann describes the psychic probe into outer space as an experiment in "out-of-body travel," suggesting *psychic* movement through space. In an out-of-body experience, our consciousness appears to leave our physical body—we may see our body lying motionless below. In this extremely liberated state, travel to distant places is possible. Is this what Swann did? Perhaps, instead of "traveling," Swann expanded the range of his awareness beyond the bounds of his body and near vicinity to include the distant planets. Or perhaps he saw into the future, and examined the reports of the NASA spacecraft as they were analyzed by scientists. Either interpretation assumes a considerable psychic feat. Yet how we imagine the operation of psychic awareness will prove quite important.

## BECOME AN INSTANT PSYCHIC

Imagine, if you will, that you can take a pill that will make you instantly psychic. Suddenly, you are able to experience the world from the point of view of people nearby; you know their thoughts, feel their feelings. What would that be like?

In a study conducted by Charles Tart, Ph.D. (a psychology professor at the University of California at Davis and a long-time researcher of psychic phenomena), a group of college students and residents of a community in California were asked to contemplate taking such a pill. Their reactions were mostly negative.

The most frequently expressed worry concerned lack of control—people were afraid of becoming overloaded, of being continually bombarded with information from other people's minds. One person thought that he would pick up on other people's dreams and not be able to sleep. Many expressed concern about such negative side effects as being driven crazy by the experience, and needing to retreat to a place of solitude. Others worried about being confused—not knowing how to tell whose thoughts they were getting, or—even worse—not being able to distinguish their own thoughts from those of others. That possibility was particularly scary.

Have you ever walked into a roomful of people and felt the "bad vibes" in the room? During meetings at work, for example, you can tell that something is wrong—people are upset, something is not right. That's almost like mind reading. Would you like to know more, to be even more psychic in a situation like that? What would that be like? The following imaginary account of a mind-reading experience, inspired by Dr. Tart's "pill," illustrates what might happen:

I look over at Martha, and I begin to feel her anger. Now I can also hear her thoughts, the cursing and the accusations that are going through her mind. As I tune in more closely, I feel the frustration behind the anger—the hurt feelings and the disappointment. I also experience some of her memories, and understand the personal context that is making this frustration so important at this particular meeting. The patterns in her life, how she dealt with frustrations and anger in the past, and how her self-esteem was affected by frustrations—all this flashes into my mind.

I also tune into her body. Her heart is pounding faster, and I can feel the heart pressing against the resistance in the arteries that are clogged with cholesterol. I can sense her blood pressure rising. I get an image that, somewhere down the road, a heart attack is in store for her as a result of the food she eats and her patterns of frustration and anger. My heart goes out to her, and I wish that she could relax. But I also sense her fear. Relaxing at this moment would seem threatening. She doesn't want to lower her defenses, so she feels trapped in her cage of anger and resentment. I know all this and more in a split second.

My eyes move to Bob, sitting next to Martha. I can see what his life is like, and how it affects him in this meeting. But just then Fred begins to speak, and the tone of his voice expresses volumes of information—in the pitch and the rhythm of his speech I can sense his nervousness and his attempt to take control of a sticky situation; from the tentativeness and forced gentleness of the words I can hear how he is attempting to deal with stress.

So while I am looking at Martha's face and seeing her life unfold before me, I am also experiencing the sounds of Fred's voice, and his life is also unfolding before me. It is a bit confusing, to say the least. I want to regain some focus, as I have my own business to bring up and feelings to express about this meeting. But with all this other information I'm getting about the people in the room, I know that I will feel the impact of my own behaviors and viewpoints upon their goals, desires, and feelings. I just don't know how I'm going to be able to process all this and still function at my own job. I'm going to try to tune out some of the noise and focus on my own objectives.

This person feels overwhelmed and confused. Concentrating so much on the feelings of other people makes it difficult to stay in touch with his own thoughts and goals. Fortunately, he is making an attempt to take control by focusing the gift and turning down some of the input. Knowing what the other people at the meeting are thinking and feeling tends to inhibit action and makes the person a bit more cautious, less willing to do what is in his own self-interest. Such a concern for others could be a deterrent to the competitive spirit!

A telepathic connection to people around you would certainly affect your relationship with them. Almost half the people in Dr. Tart's study expressed some doubt about their ability to handle such telepathic information maturely. What if they heard thoughts that they weren't supposed to know? Would they be able to resist taking advantage of someone whose thoughts they knew? What if they heard unkind thoughts about themselves, things that hurt their feelings, things they wish they hadn't heard? What would they do then?

One man confessed to having a lot of nasty, mean, selfish thoughts, thoughts that might cause him to be rejected or to become the target of ridicule should other people become aware of them. It feels good to be loved in spite of our negative aspects, he said, but he wasn't so sure that he would be able to love people no matter what they were thinking. Others confided a similar worry. They wouldn't want their own thoughts read, and were not so sure that it was fair to read someone else's thoughts. To some it seemed like an invasion of privacy; others were concerned with encountering thoughts that might prove troublesome or upsetting. Mind reading could lead to concern over what other people think, which is already a problem for many people.

Some people had positive responses as well, although

they were less specific. Dr. Tart pointed out that the most frequently mentioned positive remark was that mind reading would be "interesting," or something similarly vague. The most specific positive reaction was that mind reading might improve communication through increased empathy. One person suggested that by reading other people's thoughts you could come up with a lot of ideas that you'd never think of yourself—"you'd be a genius in no time."

Are you surprised at the results of the survey, or sympathetic with the concerns? It is interesting that the people in the study were more likely to imagine negative consequences than positive ones, and to describe them in such vivid terms. Clearly, the negative side of psychic awareness seemed more real to them than the positive side. This response could have been due to the way the proposition was worded, of course, but this study is not the only source of evidence available that points to a fear of ESP. The fear seems to be real. In the course of this book, as we develop our psychic awareness, we will examine the sources of these fears and learn an approach that will help to overcome them.

Few people in Dr. Tart's study had much to say about the positive use of psychic awareness. Instead, they envisioned themselves as passive victims of unscreened information. Perhaps it was because the ability was thrust upon them suddenly, with no time to prepare themselves for a new way of experiencing the world. Unfair as it may seem, psychic ability can appear in just that way. Consider the case of Peter Hurkos.

Peter, a Dutch housepainter, was a member of the Netherlands' underground resistance to the Nazis during World War II. In his autobiography, *Psychic,* he describes how one day he fell from his ladder thirty feet to the ground. As he fell, his life flashed before his eyes. The last thing he remembers is the cry, "I don't want to die!" The next thing he knew, he was in a hospital. The doctor told him that it was a miracle he had survived such a severe head injury.

Later that day, Peter noticed another patient in a bed nearby. To his astonishment, he found that he knew all about this man. But he was a stranger! How was it possible? When the nurse examined Peter, he discovered that he knew things about her. When another patient said goodbye and wished him well, Peter found he was overcome with fear for him. He blurted out a warning to be careful. Peter shouted out that the man was a British agent and had been found out by the Germans and was to be killed. Two days later, the man was killed.

Peter was confused by these impressions, which had come spontaneously with the conviction of truth. When he went home four months later, he hid in his room with his "curse," refusing to come out. He was bombarded with visual impressions that made him very quiet and very afraid. He was finally drawn out by an inexplicable urge to read the Bible. He realized there wasn't one in the house, and he had to go out and buy one. As he read, he began to feel better about his condition. He found that his power was increasing, and also troubling him less. He discovered that he had what he terms the "power of faith." He decided to go out and rejoin his colleagues in the underground movement. There he found he could turn his "curse" into a "gift," by aiding in the war effort in a unique way: one of his first accomplishments was to identify Nazi spies within the underground community. After the war, he developed his psychic ability to solve crimes and locate missing people.

## PSYCHICS VIEW THEIR ABILITY

Being able to relate his psychic ability to biblical stories helped Peter Hurkos to conceive of it as the "power of faith." Being able to put his psychic ability to good use made it possible for him to value his gift and to develop it further. Like the subjects in Dr. Tart's survey, Peter was confronted with the sudden appearance of acute psychic sensitivity. Just as the subjects imagined, Peter experienced himself as an overwhelmed victim of an ability he could not control. Only when he developed a new perspective on his psychic gift, which gave him a sense of purpose and the ability to direct it toward specific goals, was it possible for Peter to have positive feelings about psychic awareness.

In *Many Voices: The Autobiography of a Medium,* the psychic Eileen Garrett describes how she, too, wondered about the nature of her ability and its source. Her psychic ability appeared suddenly, at a seance she was attending. She spontaneously went into a trance and a "spirit" spoke through her. People seemed to be helped by what the "spirits" that spoke through her offered. She spent the rest of her life investigating the nature of her psychic ability. Near the end of her life, she realized that she most valued her psychic gift just because of what it taught her about her true, inner nature.

Edgar Cayce was also an involuntary psychic, and he struggled against his gift until he realized that it could help people. The human side to his story is well told in Thomas Sugrue's biography, *There Is a River.* Cayce had lost his voice because of a paralysis of his throat muscles. After seeking treatments by several doctors and being diagnosed as incurable, he tried hypnosis. Under hypnosis, Cayce spoke in a normal voice. In one session, he diagnosed the condition himself and developed a cure. Hearing of this accomplishment, someone asked Cayce if he could—under hypnosis—diagnose and prescribe a cure for their daughter, whom doctors had not been able to treat. Cayce tried it and was successful.

For some time, Cayce was suspicious of his "sleeping" talent, afraid that it might be a sign of devilish influences. Although he didn't like being a "freak," the fact that he seemed to be able to help people with their problems finally convinced him that he should persist in his efforts. All his life, however, he questioned the source of this ability and its meaning. In some of his trances, he was asked about his psychic ability. The information that came helped him to bridge the gap between his down-to-earth, traditional Christian belief system and the infinite riches that seemed to lie dormant within his unconscious. Thus his psychic awareness led him on an investigation into greater self-realization. It was that search for the meaning of his psychic gift that provides the basis of this book.

When we study the lives and insights of other psychics, as Cayce suggested we do, we discover a common theme. It is this: that psychic ability is best used not for personal profit, but to help others and to learn more about oneself.

## STUDENTS OF PSYCHIC ABILITY EXPRESS THEIR FEARS

It is not just the gifted and accomplished psychics who confront doubts and fears concerning their psychic ability. Ordinary people who deliberately set out to develop psychic ability, even under experienced guidance, also run into such obstacles. Consider, for example, the results of another study by Dr. Tart.

In this study, Dr. Tart interviewed people involved in a psychic development training seminar. They were students of Helen Palmer, a professional psychic in Berkeley, California, who is so much in demand that her waiting list for appointments is over a year long. Her students had primarily positive feelings about their psychic development; but when they were questioned concerning their fears, they shared a number of revealing observations.

Most were concerned about opening up to the unknown. They feared a loss of control, and worried about becoming possessed or taken over by an outside influence. Many feared losing control of their life in general and asked, "Will I ever be able to get back to normal?"

As the psychic opens to other realities, things can get confusing. Previous bases of security can be threatened. Knowing what is "real" and what is "not real" is very important to one's sense of stability. Once-familiar boundaries no longer provide secure comfort. Yet the psychic still has to live in the consensual world—what we call the "real world"—and sometimes a psychic is afraid of getting hurt by being so open. The feeling of being different can create a sense of isolation; and the inability to communicate their experience, or sensing that their communications frighten other people, can further alienate psychics.

Psychics typically perform services for others, and this activity brings up other fears concerning loss of control. For example, having to depend upon other people for validation ("Am I crazy, or does my reading seem meaningful to you?") and not always getting it. When other people are critical or skeptical, it can create confusion and self-doubt for the psychic. It is frightening to realize that one depends for validation upon people whose own problems prevent them from recognizing the validity of one's psychic information.

Interacting with people on such an intimate level can raise other control issues. The psychic may be concerned about becoming contaminated with the other person's problems, getting sick or emotionally upset. This concern forces the psychic toward continual self-examination and self-development.

In addition to concerns about control, psychic ability raises issues of power, ethics, and evil. Feeling people's negative thoughts toward you stimulates a desire to respond in kind, but powerful energies are involved. It can be frightening and tiresome.

Exploring the outer edges of familiar reality can be scary, even for those who are accustomed to doing so. It involves a transformation of self that makes it a grow-or-perish situation. As one psychic put it, "You don't work on yourself in order to become a better psychic reader, you work on being a psychic reader in order to work on yourself."

In examining these statements from developing psychics, we can first note the repetition of the concern about loss of control that we encountered with the subjects who were simply imagining what it might be like to be psychic. Perhaps their imagination tuned into something real.

Second, we can notice the concern about being different, or seeming weird or frightening to others. These concerns express a feeling of loneliness. In his autobiography, Ingo Swann wrote,

I have never said it before, but as awareness begins to become less dependent on sensory perceptions and one begins to be aware of other magnitudes, it is possible to come to the threshold of a type of loneliness native to the psychic state. It is a brand of loneliness characterized by a sort of beautiful sadness; one can sense that all beings probably experience it at one time or another.

Some are fascinated by this; others recoil and refuse to hear about it. This special loneliness seems to have many levels of emotion within it, and in art as well as life it can be dramatized through many artificial conditions—through sex, food, thinking, all the things some people do in excess to try to hide the beautiful sadness of their intuited loneliness.

To simply know or be familiar with oneself and others as bodies is not enough to many people. Yet to reach out mentally, emotionally, or psychically to touch the being of others always seems a risky business because the searcher himself collides with the wall of loneliness. People aware of themselves as more than mere physical bioelectrical systems, aware of more than just eating, fornicating, aging and dying bodies, run headlong into the isolation imposed upon them as a result of the obiter dictum that holds that, if a person feels he is more than just body, he is wrong. (*To Kiss Earth Goodbye*, pp. 65–66)

Ingo learned early in life not to share his experiences with others. In his youth, he made a conscious decision to stop the "traveling" he had grown to love so much, and gradually his psychic facility faded into the background. It wasn't until he was an adult, living in a community that was interested in psychic phenomena, that he allowed it to reemerge. Accounts of children who were taught that their psychic perceptions were wrong are fairly common. These children soon learn to suppress their awareness in order to avoid criticism, scorn, and rejection.

A third concern expressed by the psychics in Tart's study is fear of contamination. As the boundaries between the psychic and other people are reduced, the psychic begins to want some way to keep the other person out. Edgar Cayce experienced this problem. Those who were around him on a daily basis learned how their moods would invariably affect him, much to their chagrin and embarrassment. His associates served as buffers for Mr. Cayce. They kept the people who came to him for help at a distance, so that he would not be affected by their moods. Harmon Bro, in *Edgar Cayce on Religion and Psychic Experience,* observed that although Cayce was a compassionate and caring person, he nevertheless often engaged people in only light conversations or entertained them with stories, as a means of keeping himself from being affected by their moods. Here he had developed a means of controlling the fact that the boundary between him and others was very weak.

Finally, note Tart's concluding observations: developing psychic awareness involves some sort of transformation of self; the psychics decided that if they were going to survive it, they should look at it as a means of personal growth. Although it is very important to consider what you will do with your psychic ability, it seems even more important to consider first what the ability will do with *you!*

## THE VALUE OF EDGAR CAYCE'S APPROACH TO THE DEVELOPMENT OF PSYCHIC AWARENESS

Developing psychic abilities can indeed take us into ponderous situations. Loss of control, loss of a stable sense of self, loss of secure boundaries between yourself and the people around you, loss of limits on your sense of power, and loss of confidence in what is reality—these are no small matters. What will replace the sense of lost control? If the old self-concept is lost, what concept of self will replace it? If boundaries between you and others are dissolved, how will you discriminate between what is right for you and the needs of others? If you discover new, unlimited power within yourself, what will you do with your negative feelings? If you cannot trust "reality," what can you trust?

In the face of such concerns, which arise naturally during the development of psychic awareness, the perspective offered by the Edgar Cayce readings promises comfort, security, and a positive direction. To begin, it might be helpful to compare what you imagine it is like to be psychic with the vision of psychic ability provided by Cayce.

Psychic awareness seems, at first, way out of normal experience. As much as we might like such a gift, it nevertheless seems to be an oddity, like the awesome powers of the cartoon superheroes. Cayce, on the other hand, would have us stretch our imagination to realize that psychic awareness is part of our natural endowment. It is an ability that has been forgotten and needs to be remembered, not something new that needs to be added. We are already psychic. We use our psychic ability daily, although only minimally and usually unconsciously. Learning to use our psychic abilities in a conscious manner can help us, not only in daily life, but to awaken to our true identity as companions of the Creator.

As you begin to become conscious of psychic awareness, your self-identity will change. The fear described by the psychics is a signal from your old self, warning you that your accustomed identity is being threatened. Psychic awareness, imagined from the point of view of your normal identity, is inherently frightening, for it threatens to extinguish that identity. Before we try to develop conscious psychic awareness, Cayce would have us first prepare ourselves to accept a new identity. He would have us develop an awareness of our spiritual identity, one that is based on nonmaterial, infinite, and eternal components, to supplement our personal identity, which is fixed within the body. It is much easier for a consciousness rooted in a spiritual identity that exists beyond the constraints of time and space to accept the functioning of psychic ability as a natural talent. Not only does such a shift in identity make psychic functioning more natural, but it provides us with other needed benefits as well.

Being psychic means that the boundaries we have set

up between ourselves and others will fall. We have seen how scary that can be. Cayce suggests that when we prepare to become psychically aware, we think about the nature of our relationships with other people. If we can identify with our spiritual being, we will realize that we are intimately connected at the spiritual level with all other beings. At that level, there are no boundaries. We then discover that we are not alone in this world, not cut off from nature and the people around us.

Boundaries protect us, but we pay for that protection. Many of us experience anxieties as we wonder how we will survive the threats to our existence, our livelihood, our concept of who we are and what we need in this competitive world. It's hard to grow up and have to learn what you need to know and do in order to survive. The world expects so much of us; there is so much to learn and we have to work so hard to compete for what we want. Realizing our spiritual identity, and the psychic awareness that comes with it, can put an end to such worries. It shows us that we already have all we need within ourselves: life itself, with the Creator as its source and being. The issue of "loss of control," which figures so largely in Dr. Tart's studies, becomes less of an issue. Trust in life replaces a need to be in control.

It is much like what happens to people who undergo a near-death experience. In these cases, through an accident or surgery, the person comes close to death, or perhaps is even clinically dead for a few minutes. Many people who go through such an experience report encountering intense light, meeting loving "spirits," and getting a glimpse of a heavenly existence. Returning reluctantly to the land of the living, these people find that they no longer fear death. Consequently, they no longer fear life, but can accept it and love it more fully. Often, as in the case of the woman portrayed in the movie *Resurrection*, they return with psychic abilities.

Psychic awareness, in the manner Cayce would have us develop it, is meaningfully approached as a path of spiritual growth, of enlargement of the self-concept to include experiences that will help us to feel more alive, more in touch with others, more a part of life—an eternal part of a process that cannot be destroyed. In that context, our ethics and values change and our approach to life changes. We undergo a radical transformation of our lives. In this way, we can gain the same benefits of a near-death experience without having to have a close brush with death.

Loving others, being concerned for their welfare, and wanting to serve them—these altruistic attitudes appear more spontaneous and natural and less like moral injunctions; more like "wants" and less like "shoulds." Such a shift in attitude alleviates fears about the ethical implications of psychic ability. It is much easier to handle telepathic intimacy when we feel loving toward others than when we are suspicious or afraid. Love replaces the need for power.

Preparing the way by building a proper foundation ensures that the development of psychic awareness becomes a natural expression of an enlightened consciousness—one that is willing, ready, and able to fulfill the purpose of this dimension of life. To our ordinary personality, psychic awareness is like having a tiger by the tail. To a personality that has realized the reality of its spiritual being, psychic awareness is a natural expression of transpersonal consciousness. Psychic ability becomes not an end in itself, not a quest for power and ultimately a tremendous burden. Instead, it is a means of self-realization, of developing true individuality, of living life more fully, more creatively, and more in harmony with all the blessings we can share. Now, to be able to imagine that!

# 2

# ONENESS: THE PSYCHIC CONSCIOUSNESS

*As has ever been the experience of each soul; that the Law is One, the Source is One! and those that seek other than that find tribulation, turmoils, confusion.*

EDGAR CAYCE reading no. 1297–1

*I truly believe that we are all bound together as though we were enveloped by time, as are all the various aspects of nature. The river of my life has flowed above and below the surface toward healing, aiding, and helping other people's needs, which I appear to know below the level of the conscious mind.*

EILEEN GARRETT

EDGAR CAYCE'S APPROACH TO developing psychic ability can be expressed in this very simple formula: live the life of Oneness. That is a tall order, but so is the goal: to be able to experience psychic awareness in its most natural and perfect expression, universal consciousness!

Cayce, a down-to-earth and practical man, knew that such a statement as "live the life of Oneness" takes us in too many directions at once. How can we know where to start? When Cayce was asked that question by a small group of people who wanted to become psychic, he gave them the answer one step at a time. He required them to apply each step and make it a part of their daily lives before going on to the next step. In chapter eleven we will go over all the steps, but for now it will be simpler to begin at the beginning.

The first step is this: learn to cooperate. This may sound too easy to be useful, but it is profound in its simplicity. Cooperation means operating in coordination with others. To learn to cooperate is to make our behavior in harmony with a very basic level of the reality of Oneness, rather than to insist on "my way." Cooperation builds the consciousness of Oneness and makes it real by expressing it. Our opportunities to choose cooperation are endless, and the choices that we make at such moments are usually quite revealing of our attitude toward Oneness.

Learning to cooperate as a means of developing psychic ability might seem irrevelant, too minor a step, or too slow. I certainly know that feeling! It's hard to be patient—I want psychic ability *now*. I want to learn a technique that will give me instant telepathic impressions. Or maybe it reminds you of your youth, when you wanted to learn about sex but were told about love instead. That's great, you may have thought, but what about "doing it"? It probably wasn't until some years later, after "doing it" a lot, that you began to appreciate how sex really is about love and making love.

In the same way, psychic awareness really is about the consciousness of Oneness, and cooperation is a good place to begin. Author Lawrence LeShan agrees. In his theoretical analysis of psychic phenomena, *From Newton to ESP,* he concludes that people who have a cooperative relationship will be the most likely to experience extrasensory perception (ESP) between them. (You will find an experiment in cooperation that has consistently provided useful psychic results in the final chapter of this book. By that time you'll have the tools to try the experiment yourself.)

Cayce once compared the training of psychic ability to the training of a prizefighter. He pointed out that to make a good prizefighter, you certainly would not settle for simple muscle building or simply teaching the person how to throw a punch. You would have to train the whole person, for it is the person who will use the specific techniques. The personality of the prizefighter has a big effect on his effectiveness in the ring; on the other hand, it would take an awfully big and powerful man to survive as a fighter who had no skills. Being successful requires both the development of the person and the training of skills.

For example, the most general level would be to train the fighter's personality—to be patient, to control anger, and to persevere. When we train psychic ability, we need to work on such personality traits as cooperation, empathy, and loving respect for others.

The next level for the fighter would be to train for stamina and coordination, for which exercises such as jogging and jumping rope are helpful. In developing psychic ability, meditation helps to open us up to a new style of consciousness.

Then the fighter would need to learn what stance to take—not just his arms and legs, but how psychologically to face an opponent, what strategies to use, and so on. Similarly, when we learn psychic ability, we need to learn how to recognize subtle feelings and imagery, and to be able to recall dreams.

Finally, the fighter would get specific instructions: how to throw a particular punch, how to effect certain blocks, how to move in and out of positions. In the same way, there are many specific techniques for developing and using psychic ability, which you will learn in later chapters.

When Cayce begins with Oneness as the first principle, and mentions cooperation as a good way to practice it, he is giving us a general orientation at both the philosophical and practical levels. In the same way, a street fighter who aspires to the ring might have to learn the meaning of professionalism—to learn not to take certain things personally and not to let his ego get in the way.

# ONENESS AS THE FIRST PRINCIPLE

Imagine you have no head. That's right, look at the world around you, but pretend that you have no head. Imagine that your body stops at your shoulders. You are no longer seeing with your eyes or your rational mind. Let the world you see take the place of your head. Now the world is your head!

This odd experiment in entering an altered state of consciousness comes from D. E. Harding's book on meditation, *On Having No Head,* and is meant to help us experience the world in a new way. Practice it a bit. As you look about, try to pay attention to the fact that even though you have no head, you still have awareness of the world. Where is that awareness? Can you locate it? The situation will seem to change from the normal state of "I have awareness," to "Awareness is." Welcome to the reality of awareness, of "mind at large."

As you forget about your head, you open up out into the world and the world joins you and becomes you. You are still aware of individual objects—the single flower, the squirrels—but each is somehow connected to you, for the world is no longer blocked off from you by your head.

Ordinarily, we each perceive ourself as separate from the world, and so we are free and can walk about within the world. This feels good, but it has a down side. When you see yourself as separate, you'll experience yourself as a single and separate life that needs protection in order to survive. You become alienated from the world by that sense of separateness. But when you experience yourself as having no head, as having the world as your head, you and the world are somehow connected. You can experience yourself as "one with" the world.

Cayce repeatedly expressed his concept of Oneness in his readings. All and everything is as One. When he emphasized the law of Oneness, he was reiterating what is known as the "Perennial Philosophy," a term invented by Gottfried Leibniz, the inventor of calculus, and made popular by Aldous Huxley in his book of the same title.

The Perennial Philosophy is the core message of all religions: behind all the diverse, visible manifestations of the world there lies a unitary Supreme Being—"That art Thou."

According to the Perennial Philosophy, all of creation is interconnected. Although everything appears to be separate, there really are no separate entities. Each is an inherent part of the whole. For example, each ocean wave appears to be a separate "thing," but waves are in fact passing expressions of the ocean. Each wave is one with the ocean.

Behind appearances lies a unitary reality, a Supreme Being. The Supreme Being is considered to be visible and immanent, and at the same time invisible and transcendent. This can be a bit confusing to comprehend if we approach it on a rational level.

According to the Perennial Philosophy, consciousness and the material world, or "inner" and "outer," are one and the same. The Supreme Being, or Kingdom of God, is within you as well as outside of you. We commonly think of life as being made of mind and matter; but mind and matter are in fact two aspects of the same one reality. That reality is *you*. You are that creation, that all-in-oneness called life. At the very least, the Perennial Philosophy suggests that there is more to you than you might suspect based solely on your sensory impressions of the world around you.

We can find the principle of Oneness in the Judeo-Christian Bible, where Jesus says, "The first [commandment] is, 'Hear, O Israel: The Lord our God, the Lord is One; and you shall love the Lord your God with all your heart, and with all your soul, and with all your mind, and with all your strength.' The second is this, 'You shall love your neighbor as yourself.' There is no other commandment greater than these" (Mark 12:29–31). Typically, the statement "the Lord is One" is taken to mean that there is only one God, or one Creator. That is certainly one of the meanings. But it can also mean that all of creation is one, and that one is God. Rather than imagine God as a being who lives up in the sky, imagine

God as an infinitely large being, and the earth and all its inhabitants as one atom in God's body.

The commandment to "love your neighbor as yourself" is usually taken to mean be good to others as you would like them to be good to you. As you want to be loved, love others. If you want respect, show the other person respect. In other words, the best way to treat someone else is the way you would like to be treated yourself—the Golden Rule. A deeper understanding is that your neighbor *is* yourself. If creation is one Supreme Being, then everything in creation is a piece of that being.

The concept of Oneness may seem strange at first, but it is essential to the understanding of psychic ability. As we go on, we'll see some evidence that the Perennial Philosophy is perhaps more than a philosophy; it may just be the way things are—which makes psychic ability a natural part of the real world.

## ECOLOGY: ONENESS IN NATURE

Ecology is a modern concept that reflects the image of unity in creation. We hear a lot about ecology these days, in terms of pollution, the extinction of various species of wildlife, the sustainability of life on earth. Ecology defines all living systems as interdependent. One organism's input depends upon another's output. Thus animal life needs oxygen and gives off carbon dioxide, whereas plant life needs carbon dioxide and gives off oxygen.

Ecology also holds that the various life systems are interconnected: if you change one element, you will change them all, setting in motion a chain reaction. Almost too late are we realizing the implications of this fundamental ecological principle. For example, we kill insects we don't like with sprays. The chemicals get into the earth and poison the food chain. Without those insects certain other insects thrive beyond nature's intention, while certain birds are cut off from their food and die off. With fewer birds to carry seeds to other parts of the country, pollination is threatened and fewer plants reproduce. Crop yields are affected, and farmers frantically add more amendments to the soil. The quality of the soil is affected, and trees fail to thrive. With fewer trees around, more homes are exposed to the sun and there is more need for air-conditioning. When freon gas leaks out of air-conditioners, it rises into the upper atmosphere where it destroys the ozone layer. With the ozone layer diminshed, more of the sun's harmful radiation penetrates to earth, making life less livable. And so on. The planet's life system, in all its interdependent parts, functions as a whole. According to geochemist James Lovelock, whose book *Gaia: A New Look at Life on Earth* has been highly influential in this regard, the earth is a living entity.

Thinking about ecology is a good beginning toward being able to imagine the concept of Oneness. It's an especially good image because of its connotations of respect for the earth. The image of ecology prompts us to feel concern and respect for everything on the planet—the same sort of reverence implied by the Perennial Philosophy, and the same attitude Cayce has in mind for us as we begin to explore psychic ability. Cayce's approach to ESP is definitely not value-free, but has its foundation in respect for the Oneness of all life.

## QUANTUM PHYSICS DISCOVERS ONENESS

When physicists began to look deep within the atom, they set off a chain of discoveries that have totally transformed our view of the world, of creation, even of reality and the relationship between consciousness and the material world. Recently, some fascinating books on the subject have been published: Fritjof Capra's *The Tao of Physics,* and Gary Zukav's *The Dancing Wu Li Masters: An Overview of the New Physics,* among others. The titles of both books refer to Eastern metaphysics for a good reason: modern Western physics has shown reality to be much more like that described in Eastern mysticism than we previously believed. Let's look at some of these major scientific findings that pertain to the reality of "Oneness."

First of all, at the subatomic level "things" actually almost disappear. The "things" appear to be not solid, but transitory concentrations of energy. Einstein's famous equation, $E = MC^2$, which equates mass (material) with energy, proves to manifest in a situation where "thingness" practically disappears. Instead, energy patterns seem to involve probabilities that the energy will coalesce into a "thing" at a particular location at a particular time. The "thing" referred to is not an object, as we normally think of it, but a standing wave. A standing wave is a wave that is apparently stationary, but is in fact created by the coming together of two waves traveling in opposite directions. The word *wave* is a noun and thus suggests an object; but in fact it describes a process. Thus one of the discoveries of modern physics is that "things" dissolve into patterns of waves of energy. So creation, or reality, is not a collection of things, but a dance of energy patterns. It is the same body of energy, appearing in different patterns. Not only is everything on earth interconnected, everything is really the *same* thing—energy moving about and taking different forms. And that is one way to begin to imagine what is meant by the Oneness that lies behind visible creation. In mysticism and metaphysics energy is frequently a synonym for God.

According to the Perennial Philosophy, you are the whole of creation, your consciousness and the reality out there are one. Modern physics has also discovered that dimension of Oneness. The beginning of this discovery was "Heisenberg's Indeterminancy Principle" or "Uncertainty Principle." At first this principle seemed to be a straightforward limitation of the mechanisms of science, but it has led to even more paradoxes about the nature of reality and consciousness. Heisenberg's principle refers to the fact that in order to "see" a subatomic particle, one must "shine light" on it. That light is itself made up of particle waves; when the light waves hit the particle you want to look at, it bumps the particle, thus moving it. When the light bounces off the particle to return to the observer's eye, and the observer "sees" the particle, the particle has moved for having been "seen." As a result, the observer cannot be certain as to the exact location of the observed particle. The source of the uncertainty is that the observer affects the observed!

Consciousness, then, is not an innocent witness, but affects that which it becomes conscious of. As physicists explore more deeply into this puzzle, it becomes even more puzzling, since the effect of consciousness itself seems to play a key role in creating reality. As physicist Sir Arthur Eddington put it, "The stuff of the world is mind-stuff." We are not able to see reality, per se, but what we experience is the result of our approach to observing it. Some go so far as to say that there is no reality beyond that which our consciousness creates. This dimension of Oneness, although familiar to the mystic and metaphysician, has proved to be one of the most radical results of modern subatomic physics.

Cayce also provided several images of the workings of creation that seem to have anticipated the findings of quantum physics. In particular, he described the "rotary forces" within the atom as being of primary importance, a concept that proves important in one of the recent discoveries of physics. (It will also play a role later in this book, when we explore Cayce's concept of the glandular system as a receiver of psychic energy.) Modern physics has discovered that the underlying unity of consciousness and matter has a very special dynamic property: between its various parts there can be instantaneous communication over vast distances, faster than the speed of light. The experiment involved observing the spin on a subatomic particle—the "rotary force" deep within.

As we have seen, the act of making an observation affects the results. In this case, the spin on a particle depends upon how you observe it. Potentially, its spin can be along any axis. But once the observer chooses one axis to consider, the spin is observed to be around that axis, going either "up" (clockwise) or "down" (counterclockwise). In certain situations, particles are emitted in pairs, and it is found that they have opposite spin. No matter what axis is chosen as a basis for measurement for the first particle of the pair, once its spin is measured along that chosen axis, the other particle of the pair will be found to be spinning along the same axis, but with opposite spin.

Einstein proposed separating a pair of particles that are spinning in opposite directions. Years later, when the experiment was carried out, it was discovered that the spin link between the two particles was instantaneously maintained, even over great distances. It would seem that some form of extrasensory communication exists between subatomic particles! Most physicists have not been willing to concede that this is a form of ESP, but grappling with this surprising phenomenon has led them to propose profoundly mystical models of the nature of reality.

Thus quantum physics has come upon the mystery of Oneness as expressed in the Perennial Philosophy. Before the advent of subatomic physics, it was hard for Western minds to imagine in any concrete fashion the meaning of Oneness; but now we have specific scientific findings upon which to fix the imagination. Some have cautioned that the results of quantum physics do not "prove" the Perennial Philosophy. Yet these results have certainly confounded our normal view of the world and made the concept of Oneness seem less far-fetched, less "mystical," and more grounded in reality.

## AN EXPERIMENT IN AWARENESS

Perhaps the phrase "That are Thou" can now take on new meaning for us. Let's take off our heads and contemplate this for a moment.

The world is you, and all the world is God. You, then, are the world. As another saying has it, "Be still, and know, I am God." That is said to be the voice of the "I am" presence within us, the God that is within us. You might object, saying you are not as big and powerful as God, that to think such a thing is the opposite of religious humility. But don't think about it, experience it;

let the still, small voice speak to you. When we think about it our little self takes a hold of that concept and says "Who me? *I* am God?" But the Perennial Philosophy is not addressed to your little self, but to the larger Self that dwells within.

To get a better feeling for that larger Self, perhaps to reacquaint yourself with it, consider the following exercise. Visualize a word or a picture in your mind. Focus on it. Don't let it change, don't let your mind wander. As you fix your attention on this inner image you will notice that your mind occasionally wanders in spite of your intentions, and you leave your focus to think about other things. If you were observant, you could say to yourself, "Now I am thinking of this (something else), now my focus has changed." Most times, however, the change in focus or straying of concentration happens and continues for a while before you become aware of it. Also, as you try to keep focused on that single image or word, you'll notice that it changes, transforms into something else, moves around, or does anything but remain perfectly still and constant. Keep trying to fix your attention on that one image or word, and don't let it change. As you do so, you will become aware that the "I" that is trying this experiment is not the only life within you. There must be some other source of will that distracts your attention or changes the object on which you are trying to focus. In spite of your efforts to fix your attention, another will changes things around. When you realize that you are not "single-minded," make the effort to dominate the situation, to keep your attention riveted to an unchanging focus. You will become aware that it takes an effort, that it is somewhat of a struggle. You can only succeed for a few moments at a time, and it is tiring.

Now become aware that there is more inside you than simply your sense of "I" that is trying to stay focused on that image, and that "other" that keeps things changing. Yes, there is that struggle between what seems like two parts, but in the background is another awareness, an observer who has recorded all that happened. It was aware. Simply aware, it engaged in no struggle, it took no sides, it felt no frustration as the focus was lost, it felt no relief as the focus was surrendered. It had no feelings, but it took it all in. You can feel it there, sense it as a background awareness. Some have called it the Fair Witness or the Silent Witness, and some call it pure awareness. If you tune into it, if you can sense the quality of its awareness, perhaps you will feel something familiar about it. Yes, it was there during the entire experiment, even though you weren't always aware of it. It was always aware, you can sense that. Perhaps you can also sense that is a more permanent part of you, a more unchanging part, than is the "I" part that tries to direct things, or of the parts of you that you wish to direct. It is simply awareness.

That awareness is a more appropriate candidate to respond to the word "I" in the statement, "Be still, and know, I am God." That awareness is closer to what is being addressed as "Thou" in the statement, "That are Thou." When you address that awareness and tell it that it is one with the "I" of God, the awareness doesn't grab onto the idea and run with it, entertaining all sorts of fantasies about its greatness, nor does it reject the idea as repugnant. Instead, it is accepting, witnessing, unchanged. This awareness is not to be equated with God, but it is more aligned with the meaning of the Perennial Philosophy than our "I" that thinks about it. We are not always tuned into the presence of that awareness, but it is always aware of us. Likewise, God is always aware of that awareness within us, but that awareness is not always tuned into the presence of God within it. But it can be: for the presence of God within that background awareness is always ready for discovery, just as that awareness is always present to the I consciousness, if it will but tune into it. As the promise goes, "Be still, and know."

It is that background awareness which needs to be addressed in some of these concepts. The "I" that you normally relate to has a hard time dealing with the concept, but that other awareness can deal with it, can learn and profit from it. Just as you can be awakened to the background awareness (for example, by always being alert and saying to yourself, "Now I am aware of this, now I am aware of that . . .") so that background awareness can be awakened to something that enfolds it, and thus its awareness can be enlarged.

To conclude this demonstration, try taking off your head again and experiencing the world. Pick out an object and look at it. Notice how your consciousness of that object feels to you. Now notice how your inner awareness, the background awareness, feels to you. When you compare the feel of your background awareness to the feel of the consciousness of the object, it is hard to distinguish the two. The content may differ, but the feeling is the same. That awareness is the link between the inner you and the outer world. That awareness knows no difference between the inner world of consciousness and the outer world of objects. Awareness is all there is. You and the world are one.

Now add the final dimension that makes up the formula for psychic consciousness: love! It will bring the truth to life. Allow yourself to feel love for all that you experience. Rather than simply looking at things, examining your awareness as you ask yourself if you and that outer stuff are really one, allow yourself a feeling of love, an outpouring from your heart. It is a bridge that actively links you and the world. It joins you and the world in spirit, for love is a spirit and, in all religions, an essence of God.

## AN APPLICATION OF THE CONSCIOUSNESS OF ONENESS

A similar experiment has demonstrated the reality of psychic bonding between people. The ideas we have been discussing have practical implications for the development and use of psychic awareness.

Many psychics consider their psychic functioning to arise out of a state of consciousness different from the ordinary one. Lawrence LeShan in *The Medium, the Mystic, and the Physicist: Toward a General Theory of the Paranormal,* studied the writings of Eileen Garrett and other psychics and dubbed the state they entered *clairvoyant reality*. That state of consciousness involved a "shift in awareness" in which "illusions of present time, our situation in space, and differentiations in consciousness (individuality) are transcended." There is an experience of "fundamental unity and oneness of all things." He quotes Garrett, "I have an inner feeling of participating, in a very unified way, with what I observe—by which I mean that I have no sense of any subjective-objective dualism, no sense of I and any other, but a close association with, an immersion in, the phenomena." Another psychic, Rosalind Heywood, said of her psychic state, "All human experience is one."

When LeShan compared the statements by modern physicists with these statements by clairvoyants, he thought that their similarity was significant. He wondered if a straightforward application of the experience of Oneness was possible. It turned out that it was. By training himself in meditation, he learned how to imagine as real the clairvoyant reality of "All is one." While in that state, he attempted experiments in healing. He describes one case where he was able to help limber up the hands of an arthritic patient by simply holding her hands. When he taught others to enter this state of consciousness, he found that they were able to effect psychic healing. I think his training procedure is interesting because it shows not only that the proper use of the imagination can lead to the desired state of consciousness, but also that taking these metaphysical abstractions as true, and acting as if they were true, can lead to the anticipated results.

His training procedure took the principle of oneness at its word. He would ask one person to hold the hand of another person and stare at it. He instructed the first person to look at the hand of the other person while repeating the phrase, "This is me!" The idea was to imagine that the other person was oneself, and the exercise was a form of contemplative meditation. Whenever the mind wandered from that perception, the person was to bring it back to it. In this manner he was able to train people to elicit healing effects. If the Perennial

Philosophy is taken, not simply as a philosophy, but as a practical guide to an altered state of consciousness, it can have direct, practical effects. The theory works! It can work for you.

## IN THE APPLICATION COMES THE AWARENESS.

"Try it for yourself and see. That is the real test!" Many times Cayce warned that he did not want us simply to *believe* him. He wanted us to try out the concepts in practical ways in our everyday lives. Information is of no use except as it proves worthwhile in one's own experience, he advised. His philosophy of learning is expressed in his motto, "In the application comes the awareness." Experience is the great teacher, and Cayce taught that the higher states of consciousness, the awareness of higher truths, would come from the practice of the principles that the truths implied. If you experience Oneness, you'll automatically feel loving. If you act lovingly, you'll come to experience Oneness.

Yet the normal personality can expect to meet some significant obstacles to being psychic. Cayce advised that it is better not to jump right in to developing psychic awareness without first developing a foundation. Create a new lifestyle that won't be threatened by psychic awareness, that can handle the implications of that kind of expanded consciousness. Cayce would have us contemplate the fact of Oneness, think about it, meditate upon it, try to experience it. Even more so, he would have us live it!

Cayce took psychic ability seriously. It was not a curiosity to him, but a very significant reality. He was not trying to put us off, but rather to put us on the right path, which will help us cope with the implications of psychic awareness and use this ability constructively. He did teach a few tricks, and I'll be sharing them with you. But the most important trick he taught was how to live life as a psychic, rather than just how to have a psychic experience. The secret is to realize that the essence of being psychic isn't contained in the moment of the psychic experience, but is expressed in the life that is lived before and after that experience. A life lived in the consciousness of Oneness is a life lived psychically. Otherwise, a psychic experience is but an oddity, hopefully a mind-opener, certainly a curiosity, possibly an inspiration, all too often a burden or source of confusion, but always an oddity. That fact may be disappointing, but it is disappointing only to the impatient part of us, and that part does not really believe in the reality of psychic awareness. The part that does believe—and it is to that part that this book is addressed—can accept this truth, in patience, even if with a sigh of "Aw, shucks."

I am reminded of Native American shamans who, when asked about such powers as psychic ability, laugh at the contradiction of the question when the questioner—usually a "white eyes"—is so obviously not living the life of Oneness and respect for the planet. "How can you say that you want to learn psychic awareness," asks the Native American of the white person, "when all your life you have been so keen on ignoring the screams of the grass when you walk on it? If you really want to learn psychic awareness, first learn to walk gently upon Mother Earth and be thankful that she allows you to walk upon her at all!"

Our daily behavior and the consciousness that we wish to develop must be in accord. So, in your spare moments, take off your head, and experience the world from the point of Oneness. And all the rest of the time, experiment with cooperation, to see where it will lead you in your awareness. Mother Earth may surprise you.

# 3

# THE IMAGINATION OF THE PSYCHIC: PATTERNS OF VIBRATIONS

*Life in its manifestation is vibration.*
EDGAR CAYCE reading no. 1861–16

*There is an instinct for rhythmic relations which embraces our entire world of forms.*
FRIEDRICH NIETZSCHE

**A PSYCHIC WHO HOLDS** an object while trying to locate a lost person may well say, "I'm tuning into the vibrations." Such a statement explains how many psychics imagine their ability operates. Novelist Upton Sinclair entitled his book about telepathy *Mental Radio*. What a succinct image to express the psychic experience of tuning into vibrations! But it raises a very perplexing question: How can vibrations, which we typically associate with physical energy, convey information about a distant person's experiences?

Cayce's answer was that "thoughts are things" and, like other things, have their own vibrations. Such vibrations exist in a dimension outside of time and space. Psychic awareness is the ability to tune into these vibrations and translate this resonance into a form accessible to the conscious mind.

To understand this kind of language, which is quite common among psychics, we need to go back to some first principles. Cayce envisioned the world in a manner different than we ordinarily do, and spoke about it in terms different from our scientifically influenced language. We will need to learn how to imagine the world in the way that psychics do if we are going to develop psychic awareness.

## THE VOCABULARY OF ONENESS

Do ideas exist before we think them? If so, *where* do they exist? For example, did the idea of a wheel exist before an actual wheel was invented? The principle of a wheel was always there waiting to be discovered. Was the idea for a wheel invented or discovered? It's a puzzling question. How does an idea get into your head? How does the idea get you to think it? What stimulates your brain to fire in a particular pattern to produce a particular idea? Whether it is telepathically picking up on the ideas in someone else's head, or making a creative discovery by allowing a new idea to come in, both involve "picking up" ideas out of "the air," or getting your brain to behave in a particular pattern that corresponds to the idea you want to have. How does an idea travel? How does an idea, which is "mental," manage to get together with your brain, which is "physical?"

Such puzzling questions arise from how we imagine the way the world works. Our very language reflects the way we understand the mechanics of the world. When we speak of an object, it has a boundary around it—it exists within a specified space. To perceive this object, light beams, sound waves, or odor molecules must travel between you and it. A sensory contact of some kind must occur, because our consciousness of separateness requires that there be links between us and the not-us in order to perceive them.

When it comes to manipulating material objects in our everyday world, our ordinary consciousness, as it has been shaped by scientific language, works fairly well. This is an atomistic perspective: everything is based on the mechanics of atoms that behave like billiard balls. It is said that science reduces all life to the action of chemistry and physics, using the atom as the basic building block. Hook a few atoms together and you have a chemical. Mix some chemicals together and you have a chemical reaction. Somewhere along the line, one of these chemical reactions makes a life form. Life forms interact, and a few lucky, but accidental, chemical reactions, create new life forms. After a while we have plants, animals, and humans. A human thought is the end result of chemical reactions in the body responding to physical and chemical events in the outside world. Everything is explained as a chain of cause-and-effect sequences involving, basically, atomic processes. Another name for the atomistic approach is a *micro* perspective, for all processes are analyzed in terms of the smallest part. But many people, even scientists, balk at using the micro perspective to explain everything.

The *macro* perspective, on the opposite end, analyzes life in terms of the most general, encompassing processes that govern the smaller ones. A macro perspective is also *holistic;* for it sees a system not as an amalgamation of parts, but as a whole, as in ecology. Recent discoveries in quantum physics have stimulated a conception of the world that is more holistically integrated, if not also paradoxical. Other fields of inquiry are also beginning to question the appropriateness of the micro perspective.

Psychic awareness is a challenge to the materialistic, atomistic conception of the world. Telepathy implies to the micro that ideas can travel through space without the need for some mechanical medium like an invisible telephone wire upon which to base the exchange of information. Yet leading-edge scientific language is gradually approaching that of psychics. Cayce's language is tailored to the reality of psychic consciousness. In the previous chapter, we learned how Cayce stressed the concept of Oneness. We also read accounts of other psychics who described how they became "one with" the object of their psychic awareness.

Cayce's description of psychic awareness reveals a macro perspective. Rather than starting with something small, like atoms, and using them to build larger things,

Cayce's language of Oneness starts with something big that permeates everything—God—and then explains how Oneness is expressed in specific, yet interconnected manifestations. These manifestations are envisioned as patterns—patterns of vibration. It is like the Buddhist notion of the "Jeweled Net of Indra," their metaphor for Oneness. At each intersection of this infinite net lies a shining jewel. Each jewel contains reflections of all the other jewels, and each of these reflections contains an infinite number of reflections, so that every point in reality reflects every other point. This Buddhist image anticipates the holographic model we will examine in a later chapter, and suggests how each part of the universe may communicate with every other part by the resonance of patterns.

Whereas our consciousness of separateness ordinarily has us focus on objects, Cayce and other psychics focus first on patterns of vibrations. The vehicle of perception is also envisioned differently by psychic consciousness. We imagine perceiving as an act of movement—sense information travels, or is carried, from the object, through a medium, to our sense apparatus. Psychic consciousness imagines the process to be that of resonance to vibrations—the psychic becomes one with the pattern of vibrations. In other words, resonance, attunement, empathy, or "tuning in" is the method by which information is transferred. As elements of a vocabulary, the terms *patterns of vibration* and *resonance* both express the macro perspective of psychic consciousness. It expresses the awareness of a pervasive, interconnected unity that underlies the apparent world of sensory separateness. To develop this psychic awareness, then, let us try to resonate with how Cayce imagines this underlying unity to manifest in patterns of vibrations.

## THE CREATIVE FORCES

Just what is this "One" that Cayce says everything is "one with," which permeates all that exists? God, Creator, Creative Forces, Energy—these are the terms he

**The yin-yang symbol**

used. In so doing, Cayce evolved a description of how God functioned as the Creator, how these creative forces brought the world into being.

At the beginning of creation, Cayce tells us, the One force began by manifesting itself in two ways: as a force of attraction and a force of repulsion. On and off, up and down, in and out, black and white, plus and minus, male and female—these are some of the variations on the motif of opposites. It is a common motif in creation stories that creation began by the dividing of the One into two. The Bible, for example, tells us that God separated Heaven and Earth, light and darkness. In India's Upanishads, the world came into being as the great cosmic egg burst into silver and gold, silver becoming the earth and gold becoming the sky. These two are polar opposites, and yet both are aspects of the same underlying unity, two sides of the same coin, as they were both created from the same One.

The yin-yang symbol, shown above, is probably the oldest expression of this concept of the primal creative process. You can look at the yin-yang symbol and see how the original One, a circle, was divided into two comet-shaped parts, each apparently spinning about the other.

Cayce indicates that it was necessary for the One to

divide into two in order to create energy. The complementarity of the two is the source of the energy. You can see the yin-yang symbol as being either a white comet against a black background, or a black comet against a white background. If you stare at it a while, you will experience a psychological impression of this energy effect: first you see the white figure eating away at the black background, then you see the black figure eating away at the white background, back and forth, back and forth. Each time you make a perceptual shift, the curve cutting through the circle changes its meaning. When you focus on the white comet, the curve that defines its tail is concave, squeezing inward. But when you look at that same point on the curve from the point of view of the head of the black comet, that curve is convex, expanding outward.

That flip-flop back and forth between the two ways of perceiving the curve is the basic dynamic of vibration, an oscillation between two opposing perspectives. Oscillation/vibration is the basis of energy. Electrical energy manifests in a similar manner, with an oscillation between the positive and negative poles. All creative energy results from this one source, from the central, universal vibration at the beginning of creation. This universal vibration exists within and permeates all other derivative vibrations.

People who have studied creativity often point to the role of opposites in the creative process. In one experiment, conducted by Yale University psychiatrist Albert Rothenberg, highly creative and not so creative people who had identical IQs and scholastic achievement were compared on the word-association test. For example, they were asked to give the first word that came to mind when they thought of "joy." Uncreative types typically said "happiness," while creative types responded with the opposite, "sadness." In *The Emerging Goddess: The Creative Process in Art, Science and Other Fields,* Rothenberg identifies creativity with "Janusian thinking," after the Roman god Janus, who could look in opposite directions simultaneously. He points to such images as the yin-yang symbol and says that simultaneous oppositions—seeing something from two opposite points of view simultaneously—are the essence of the creative spark. Thus creation in the sense of bringing the world into being, and creation as a psychological process, are seen to have an identical basis—the mind and the world are as one.

## MANIFESTATION OF CREATIVITY: ENERGY, PATTERN, FORM

My father once said that creativity felt like an itch—you are compelled to express something. I experience creativity not only as an urge, but a force. I take Cayce's term *creative forces* to describe something that actually exists, both outside of me and inside of me. It is a force that can almost be intoxicating. Being creative feels like being a dancer, alive with energy. You have a willingness to feel the energy and to move with it, to turn yourself over to the energy and to flow with it. When you begin to respond to the energy, to tune into the itch, to move with the energy that you feel, then the pattern in the creative energy begins to manifest. What at first seemed simply like a pressure begins to feel like a special type of urge, a pressure with a pattern or design to it. It takes form. It comes out of nowhere and results in a visible, patterned dance or some other specific manifestation.

A very important aspect of the creative forces is their tendency to manifest. Creativity begins as pure energy, but changes by assuming a specific pattern. As a vibrational pattern, the energy contains information. The informational pattern has a way of working itself down from the very abstract, invisible level to the concrete, material level of reality.

Cayce's favorite formula for this stepladder of creativity was, *"Spirit is the life, mind is the builder, the physical is the result."* Creativity arises first at the level of spirit—which is the pure energy from basic vibrations. These vibrations assume a pattern as they enter the mental level of reality. As the "builder," mind's major attribute is patterning. Cayce often calls the creative forces at the

mental level the "imaginative forces" because of the im-
age-making process that occurs there. It is at the level of
mind that patterns exist, often in the form of images,
giving form to the unpatterned spiritual level of vibration.

The patterns of the mind, according to Cayce, exist in
another dimension. In the traditional micro perspective,
we think in terms of a three-dimensional universe, and
assume that information is carried by a physical medium
traveling the highways of these three dimensions.
Cayce's macro perspective introduces a fourth dimension—the realm of ideas—that transcends the three-
dimensional world of time and space. An idea is everywhere and always. The fourth-dimensional character of
the mind is crucial to psychic awareness. As we shall
see, other macro theorists also define some fourth-
dimensional reality of invisible, creative patterns, of
formative "ideas," and have imagined that psychic
awareness operates through this dimension.

As the mind patterns the pure energy, it begins to
precipitate the denser vibratory patterns found in the
sensory physical world. The world of material things is
seen by the psychic consciousness as stable patterns of
vibratory energy. At the physical level, these patterns
are so stable that they appear as solid, permanent objects to the sensory consciousness.

From Cayce's point of view, tangible objects, including our bodies, are history, the visible remnants of an
earlier process of vibrational energy manifesting in stable patterns. The energy is real; the physical form is
relatively unreal. In the realm of ideas, a book is the
tangible manifestation of the idea. You can burn the
book, but you have not destroyed the ideas that formed
it. If the spirit behind the ideas is still active, the ideas
will manifest again in another book.

A startling demonstration of the way invisible vibrations can affect the shape of visible forms was created in
the 1930s by Hans Jenny, a Swiss scientist. He placed
a substance—sand, powders, liquids, or putty—on a
round metal membrane. As the disk moved in response
to various sound vibrations, the substance assumed par-

ticular shapes. The underlying reality of these shapes was in the sound vibration. By removing the material, you could remove the manifested form; yet the invisible pattern of vibration remained, awaiting the means to become visible once again. Many of the shapes resembled patterns found in nature. The photographs in Jenny's book *Cymatics* show the wide range of effects. Jenny provides an emotionally convincing demonstration of Cayce's claim that God created the forms of the universe with sound and geometry.

Cayce's macro view of creation by vibration is that the source vibrations are everywhere all at once. The infinite extent of vibration has implications for the communication involved in psychic awareness. For example, a pebble dropped into water creates a rings of ripples that expand outward in all directions. Depending on the size of the pebble and the force with which it is thrown into the water, the ripples will have either shallow or deep troughs, and will be either closely or distantly spaced. By analyzing the ripples, you can determine when, where, how big, and how hard a rock was thrown into the water. The ripples in the water are a form of vibration. The pattern of ripples gives information about the nature of the rock that was thrown in the water. Moreover, the ripples caused by the rock spread over the entire surface of the lake. Rock the "object" exists in only one place; but rock the "ripple" exists throughout the lake. Patterns of vibration create information everywhere all at once.

This macro perspective also has implications for an alternative to the micro view of cause and effect. For example, the vibrational pattern that results in the creation of a bush is everywhere in the universe; but it has come down to the physical, stable level only in specific locations where that particular species of bush is growing. All examples of that species of bush are linked by the vibrational pattern that is associated with that species. In the micro perspective, on the other hand, in the physical, atomistic form of understanding, that bush replicates itself by growing seeds that birds carry to all parts of the earth, a cause-and-effect sequence of mechanical events. However, from Cayce's point of view, all the bushes extend out from the vibrational source like spokes on a wheel. The planting of a seed only determines where the central vibratory source will manifest another spoke.

Cayce's macro approach to creation has recently been echoed in the controversial theory of Rupert Sheldrake. In his book *A New Science of Life,* Sheldrake specifically attempts to overthrow the traditional mechanistic view of life. Among his propositions is that the forms of nature are organic precipitates of guiding patterns that exist in an other-dimensional reality he terms the *morphogenetic field.* The term he uses for the process, *morphic resonance,* is the academic jargon of biology; his basic propositions, however, are almost identical to Cayce's. Sheldrake used his theory of the morphogenetic field to explain the frequent occurrence of the simultaneous scientific discovery. When an idea's "time has come," according to Sheldrake, it is literally "in the air." Many different scientists, as long as they are working with the relevant material, will begin to manifest the pattern formed by the vibrations of that idea. It is as if each scientist's work is itself material sitting on one of Jenny's cymatic disks, and each begins to resonate to the pattern of the idea, each independently coming up with the same "discovery."

## RECOGNIZING PATTERNS

"The greatest thing by far is to be master of metaphor; it is the one thing that cannot be learnt from others; and it is also a sign of genius, since a good metaphor implies an intuitive perception of the similarity in the dissimilar." This quotation, attributed to Aristotle from Steven Starker's book *F-States: The Power of Fantasy in Human Creativity,* defines creative imagination as the ability to join images on the basis of the corresponding underlying patterns. It also expresses Cayce's viewpoint on the creative potential of patterns. One of Cayce's particularly insightful approaches to many areas of life concerns the importance of perceiving patterns. He would have people look for patterns in their own lives. In dream interpretation, he would have people look at the patterns in their dreams and try to match them to patterns found in their lives. Cayce anticipated modern holistic philosophers when he recognized that we perceive meaning by correlating patterns. Cayce could describe the functioning of the body using correct anatomical terms; yet, when he wished to call attention to the meaning of that functioning, he would refer to a pattern in the person's life and correlate it with the pattern of the bodily functioning.

Cayce was an expert at recognizing and correlating patterns that were invisible to others, but we are all experts at pattern recognition. Musical melodies, rhythms, and much of what we enjoy through our senses is based on patterns. Our eyes are very keen at recognizing patterns. The pattern of triangles, for example, shown on page forty-six, gives a stunning demonstration of the eye's ability to detect patterns. As you move your eyes about the design, you become aware of suddenly appearing cascades of ever larger triangles, now in black, then in white. Our eyes immediately sense the regularities in the visual field, and we experience that sensation as the discovery of patterns moving about the page.

Paradoxically, even though we are quite good at sensory pattern recognition, traditional psychology has had the most difficulty explaining it. Take our ability to recognize patterns of sound vibrations, for example. Our ears can tell the difference between a violin and a piano even when each instrument plays the same note. That is because of qualities of the vibratory sound wave in addition to the underlying frequency. Various harmonic overtones, decay rates in the loudness of these tones, and other factors affect the quality of the sound in recognizable ways. Our ears can detect these differences. In engineering terms, a human being can analyze complex wave patterns, match them, and discriminate between different forms. That we can recognize different

**Pattern of triangles**

voices shows just how complex a vibratory pattern we can analyze.

Humans perceive patterns so easily that it may come as a surprise to you that computers have great difficulty doing it. It has taken some time to develop enough understanding of the variables in a voice pattern to teach a computer to recognize voices. Teaching a computer to recognize visual patterns has been even more difficult. Yet, in fact, it has been through the process of trying to learn how to teach computers to recognize patterns that psychology finally had to face up to its lack of understanding of this very fundamental attribute of human perception.

Having to come to terms with pattern recognition has turned theories of perception upside down. Newer theories of perception now maintain that perception is based on the imagination—that to perceive something first requires being able to imagine it. Perceptual psychologists call this a "template," a guiding image that is used to organize the incoming data. This template is our "first bet" about what it is that we are looking at. We process and organize the incoming information in terms of the assumptions of the guiding image of what is there to be perceived.

When we find discrepancies, we try another image to see if we can get a better fit between what we expected and what we obtained.

Often we allow our expectations to carry the day, and we ignore contradictory data. Proofreaders, for example, will tell you that when you are looking for spelling mistakes, you shouldn't read the material for sense. When you read for meaning, even carefully, you don't notice errors in spelling. It's as though if you can understand the sentence, then all the words must be spelled correctly. To catch spelling errors, you have to read each word and look at its spelling, not its meaning. When we listen to one another speak, we usually hear complete sentences. A tape recording of the conversation, however, would show that we skip words, leave sentences dangling, unfinished, and otherwise talk in a disjunctive fashion. Oral conversation is full of holes, but we don't hear it that way. If we did, it would be quite disruptive. It is usually efficient to perceive in terms of our expectations. On the other hand, it disguises just how much we actively shape what we perceive to fit our image of what is there to be perceived.

Numerous experiments have shown how the imagination can shape or even take precedence over perceptual information from the outer world. The earliest work in this area showed how our perceptions are often governed by our needs and interests. Buy a camera and suddenly you become aware of all the people in the world shooting pictures. When you are hungry, you notice restaurants and every person who happens to be eating something. Clearly, what we perceive is determined not only by the facts, but also by our interests. The tree a nature lover sees is quite different from the tree a lumberjack sees.

That we shape our perceptions is not just a statement about attitude, it also means just what it says: we construct our experience! A popular expression of the New Age holds that we create our own reality. That's more than a slogan, it's a fact. We create reality by the imagery we use to organize our experience. The three-dimensional world that we see is fabricated in our brain based upon an inner pattern of three-dimensional space. Our brain carries images of the world and uses those images to construct our experience. Our imagination creates blueprints; the sense impressions are but the building blocks that we can arrange in any way necessary to fit the imagined pattern.

We also know that our perception is limited by the patterns we are capable of imagining. In the history of science, many advances are attributable to leaps of perception, where the old and familiar was seen in a new way. For example, the discovery by William Harvey that the heart functions as a blood pump required that he be able to imagine seeing a pump when he looked at the throbbing heart. Prior to his new vision, people imagined that blood ebbed and flowed like the tides, based on the vision of Galen. The role of the heart, in this vision, was to transform the blood, to give its "life" to the blood. Until Harvey's new vision of the heart, no one had even heard the pulse! As Robert Romanyshyn argues in *Psychological Life: From Science to Metaphor,* in order for Harvey to make his discovery, he had to bring to his observations a new vision, to imagine something different when he watched the palpitations of the heart. Here is where the imagination is the foundation of perception. It actually governs and determines what we see. Imagination becomes reality.

It is important to recognize that images are patterns. Images sometimes play a metaphorical role in our perceptions. To "see" the heart as a "pump" is to recognize that the pattern of action of a heart is analogous to the pattern of action in a machine that transfers liquids. Understanding the heart as a pump gives new meaning to the heart, and permits us to see other facts that were hidden before. Meaning is the correlation of patterns. Metaphorical and symbolic perception is where the pattern-making role of the imagination has a very creative effect upon our consciousness.

## PATTERNS OF VIBRATIONS

Webster defines pattern as a model upon which imitations, or duplicates, can be made. Plato, on the other hand, would call pattern an "Ideal." Plato maintained that the world was an imperfect manifestation of transcendent ideals, or patterns. One such ideal is the circle. Circles come up in all sorts of situations, each one varying in the closeness of its approximation to the one original circular pattern, the ideal circle. Plato maintained that each of us, having been created within nature, has within us the influence of the ideal circle, which is why we can recognize a circle when we see one. We intuitively recognize circularity. As Plato would say, circularity is an endowment of the soul. To Plato, education was not a matter of pouring in facts, but of reminding a person of all the knowledge that was already within. Cayce and Plato had a lot in common.

Cayce's concept of ideals is quite similar to the Platonic vision. First, recognize that ideas are patterns. When Cayce said that thoughts were things, he was referring to the vibratory reality of ideas. Ideas are vibrations at the mental level. When he said that "mind is the builder," he meant that the mind is the source of ideas, or patterns, that give form to the vibrations. All the words that we associate with mental patterns—image, idea, meaning, metaphor, story—all these have the reality of vibrations, patterns of vibration at the level of the mind. To Cayce, ideals were idea patterns of the highest value: universal values like love, or universally valued patterns such as the Buddha or the Christ. To Cayce, the historical Jesus was a manifestation of a pattern, an ideal that Cayce and others have referred to as the Christ consciousness. Here we have a rather complex pattern involving consciousness of Oneness, love, forgiveness, willingness to transform and transmute; yet it is capable of existing everywhere, of being repeated, as when the spirit of the Christ consciousness begins to become the formative pattern of a person's life. Cayce stressed the importance of our coming to recognize the ideal that was governing the patterns in our lives, and to choose an alternative life if the current operative ideal did not match our highest value. Ideals manifest in the patterns of our life experiences.

Cayce's thinking on this point is almost identical to that of Carl Jung. Jung spoke of *archetypes,* universal first patterns that influence or shape our experience. He located these archetypes in a fourth dimension of reality. At one level of manifestation, archetypes pattern instincts, such as the interaction of mother and child, the instigators and regulators of aggression, and the process and stages of development. At another level, archetypes shape our experience of intangibles, such as religious themes of death and rebirth, yin and yang, and the Christ consciousness. Jung noted something that Cayce also referred to, and which various philosophers as well as certain quantum physicists are beginning to state: namely, that the same patterns in the mind that created the patterns of our thinking and imagination also created the patterns of the physical world. He noted many examples of correspondences between the patterns of spontaneous imagery arising in people's minds and the patterns in nature revealed by the microscope and telescope.

The classic example of this type of interconnection is in mathematics. Math means numbers, but it also means patterns. Amazingly, people actually invent mathematics. They think up totally new mathematical realities, geometries of imaginary spaces that exist only in the minds of gifted mathematicians. Where do these ideas come from? The same place that nature herself comes from. The human imagination is truly one with nature, and the history of mathematics has repeatedly shown that no matter how bizarre the mathematical space "invented" by an ivory-tower mathematician for his or her own pleasure and amusement, the day does finally arrive when, in another branch of science, someone finds that that bizarre mathematics perfectly describes the new dimension of nature that science has uncovered. How could such a purely imaginary invention repeatedly prove descriptive of reality if our imagination and nature's patterns did not have the same source? Mind and nature are one.

## SYNCHRONICITIES AND SYMBOLISM

How many times have you had the occasion to remark, "What a coincidence!"? Chances are it happens with some frequency. When we juxtapose one pattern with a similar pattern and perceive an overlap of meaning, a meaningful coincidence occurs. Carl Jung called this *synchronicity.* Jung's synchronicity is similar to Cayce's recognition that meaning is perceived through the correlation of patterns. Jung once described an example of synchronicity from his own life. One day he was painting pictures of images from his imagination when the mailman brought him a book on ancient Chinese divination that contained a picture just like the one he was painting. The effect of this incident was to make him feel connected by his inner work to the larger world. Synchronicities are another example of how the mind and the world are connected. Simultaneity of discovery, as discussed by Sheldrake, is an example of synchronicity.

A meaningful coincidence can exist only when it's perceived. An observer is needed to notice the coincidence. In fact, not all observers will notice it. It is an emotional reaction to a perceived pattern. The pattern is the similarity between the two realms. Obviously, the two things are not related by cause and effect. The rational mind rebels at strong coincidence, but the intuitive faculty recognizes it and embraces it.

When we are involved in a creative pursuit and let our intuition come into play, very often we are surprised by serendipitous discoveries and meaningful coincidences. Our creative activity has taken us into the Oneness of patterns, where intuitions and realities merge. The thoughts inside and the realities encountered outside come together in a meaningful pattern. The boundary and distinction between discovery and creation become blurred. Thus synchronicities play a role in the operation of intuition.

As for Jung's synchronicity experience, he noted that the vehicle of the coincidence was a book on divination. He found this significant because he viewed the process of divination to be based upon the principle of synchronicity. The varieties of "oracles" operate on the principle of alignment of patterns. You want to understand the pattern in your life, yet you cannot recognize it. You throw coins and consult the *I Ching,* the Chinese book of divination based upon sixty-four patterns in creation. You examine the pattern in the toss of the coins as they are represented in the *I Ching.* With the aid of its interpretation, and based upon your own insights, you recognize the pattern in the *I Ching* as correlated to a pattern in your life. You assume that the pattern in the *I Ching* actually reflects the pattern in your life. No causal relationship is involved. Your situation in life does not *cause* the coins to fall the way they do. Your life and the toss of the coins are *two images of the same pattern.*

Cayce recognized the occurrence of synchronicities, not only in the correspondences that obtain between different areas of life, but also in the form of opportunities. It is this particular aspect of synchronicities that Cayce recommended exploring as a means of seeking guidance in life.

# THE PRINCIPLE OF CORRESPONDENCE

Symbols convey meaning because the patterns they express can be correlated to other areas of life. Not only do synchronicities often involve correspondences with symbolic patterns, but psychic awareness often involves perception through symbolism. Earlier we mentioned that Cayce used the phrase "As above, so below" to refer to patterns at one level corresponding to patterns at another. This *principle of correspondence* also appears in the writing of Emmanual Swedenborg, a psychic who developed a theory of the levels of reality that paralleled Cayce's vision in many respects.

This principle has both a vertical and a horizontal dimension. The vertical concerns how physical reality corresponds in its forms to the patterns in the creative dimension of mind. The horizontal dimension has to do with correspondences that involve analogies, symbolism, and stories. Sometimes a psychic becomes aware of a symbol or a pattern that reflects or corresponds to a reality about a person—not all psychic perception is literal.

Patterns in the mind often have several counterparts. A psychic may not perceive your exact thoughts, but rather perceive a symbolic analogue. I have seen instances where a group of people are gathered around a psychic, hoping to get information about their personal lives, and being surprised that during the informal part of the session, the psychic will tell personal stories that seem to correspond to topics in the people's lives about which they wanted readings.

Often symbols exist in clusters. Jung's term for this was the "complex." We usually think of this word as meaning a "hang-up," because it was originally used to describe how problems tended to be interrelated. Yet the word also describes the complicated network, like the Jeweled Net of Indra, that exists between symbols. Let's take the tree symbol as an example. Related to the tree symbol—a trunk with many branches, which takes nourishment from the earth and sends it coursing through itself as sap, dead and leafless in winter, bursting into new life in spring—are the spinal cord, the flow of psychic energies in a body, the process of creation itself. Such complicated symbolic patterns as myths of creation or the Book of Revelation in the Bible are—from the viewpoint of the psychic imagination—highly descriptive of the way things really are.

To our scientific viewpoint, taking such symbolic scenarios as descriptive of reality seems ludicrous. Yet remember that science too deals in models of reality, complicated metaphors that are supposed to correspond to nature. Traditional science tends to favor the models based upon a micro perspective, while the psychic feels that a macro perspective is more appropriate. When Cayce's view of the psychokinetic aspect of meditation is discussed in a later chapter, for example, bear in mind the psychic's appreciation for the formative energy contained in symbols, and that complex symbol systems are felt to correspond to complex processes in the body.

## ATTUNEMENT: MOVEMENT IN PSYCHIC CONSCIOUSNESS

If to psychic consciousness everything is created through the effects of vibrations, then it is vibrations that psychic awareness will want to focus on. Oneness, attunement, resonance, harmony, empathy, sympathy, accordance, parallel, joined, consonance—how frequently these words appear in the statements of psychics. Cayce used many of these words repeatedly to describe the process of psychic consciousness. These words have in common a focus on the qualities of two different things interacting with one another due to their being "on the same wavelength." These words form a basic aspect of the language of psychic consciousness.

I think of these words as the "motion" words of psychic consciousness, because so often a psychic will describe an act like "going to" by use of a "tuning" word. For example, Cayce would ask for the name and address of a person requesting a reading. That would be his only "road map" for "locating" the person. He then often found himself "in the presence" of the person, and could report the surroundings he observed. It was as if he went there. When asked how he did this, he described it as a process of tuning into the vibrations of the person's name. Once that attunement was made, the information flowed.

Such terms as harmony, empathy, and resonance all have musical vibration overtones. The dynamics of such each involve the equation of sympathetic vibration. Consider this metaphor for empathy: if you "walk a mile in the other person's moccasins," the experience will convey to you (note the concept of travel, or exchange, or movement in the word "convey") the other person's feelings or perspective. To know how a person feels, empathize with that person, tune into his or her vibrations, and allow yourself to resonate. In music, if one string vibrates, and the next string is made to resemble the first in terms of length and thickness and tautness, it will also begin to vibrate. This is called *resonance*. The dynamic is based on the principle of the transference of information or meaning by having the receiver become like the sender, to pick up the vibrations of the sender.

I sometimes think of my mind as a membrane that can vibrate, or resonate to vibrations. To pick up another person's thoughts I first focus on what the person "feels like." That's something we all do, whether we realize it or not. We feel good around some people, but not others. There are certainly more vibrational patterns than good or bad, there are countless different patterns. So I focus on how the person feels to me. I am empathizing with the person, in resonance. The membrane of my mind is now resonating with their vibrational "sound." Soon I notice images forming on my mind. What was at first just fuzz, like a pile of powder on one of Hans Jenny's metal disks, begins to take shape in the form of images. The person's vibrations are beginning to impress images upon my mind. This is a simple description of telepathy based on the analysis of vibrations.

Consider, for example, ESP envisioned as "mental radio," to use Upton Sinclair's term. To tune into a station we change the characteristics of the radio so that it becomes sensitive to the vibrational frequency of that station. To leave that station and go to another, we don't have to get into our car and drive from station to station—we simply twist the dial. CBs use a similar metaphor, "leaving here," when tuning to a different frequency. We "move" from one station to another by changing the attunement to a different vibratory frequency. At the flick of a dial, we instantaneously "travel" hundreds of miles from one radio channel to another.

Or consider the case of Marcel Proust, who describes in *Remembrance of Things Past* how he was "transported" to a moment in his childhood by the taste of a biscuit. Tastes and smells can be such strong reminders of the past that they seem to carry us back in time. We aren't just recollecting memories, we are actually back in the past. Again, a change in the attunement of our mind has the effect of "moving" us from one time period to another.

## THE PSYCHIC IMAGINATION

To the psychic, the imagination is everything. The world is created through the imagination of God, and that same imaginative force is active in each of us. The imagination is the realm of patterns, patterns of vibration. Consider the implications for ESP. Ideas, or patterns of the mind, exist in a fourth dimension. They are simultaneously everywhere and always. If the basis of perception is the imagination, if sensory data is subservient to what is imagined, then ESP can function simply by attuning to vibrational patterns. Sensory contact can be a support to perception, but is not absolutely required. ESP is a more direct form of perception, one that bypasses the details of the senses.

To develop psychic awareness, therefore, it is necessary to be willing and able to imagine the world as patterns of vibration, and to imagine tuning into those patterns. The psychic imagines the world in a way that allows for psychic awareness. The psychic behaves in a manner that is consistent with that image of the way things are, and then the psychic naturally functions psychically. People who just cannot believe in the reality of psychic perception have trouble being psychic. Furthermore, as if to show that our imagination shapes our reality and we behave in a way that confirms that, studies have shown that people who do not believe in ESP actually perform worse in ESP than chance would predict: these people have to use ESP in an unconscious manner in order to make sure that their guesses are wrong!

We all are psychic, whether or not we are aware of it. Using ESP unconsciously is quite common. Our hunches and intuitions detect patterns by way of unconscious ESP. In the shadow of sleep, our dreams draw upon patterns of psychic information. In such states of consciousness, outside of our normal awareness, our psychic imagination has unlimited freedom of expression. It is to such states of consciousness that we now turn, to bring their psychic potential into our conscious awareness.

# Part II

# PSYCHIC STATES OF AWARENESS

# 4

# YOUR PSYCHIC INTUITION

*How do I know the ways of all things at the
Beginning? By what is within me.*

LAO TZU

*I know when I have a problem and have done all
I can—thinking, figuring, planning—I keep
listening in a sort of inside silence 'til something
clicks and I feel a right answer.*

CONRAD HILTON

INTUITION IS OFTEN DEFINED as knowing something without realizing why or how you know it. "Hunch" is a common synonym for intuition, as are being hit by lightning, having a light bulb light up inside your head, having everything fall into place, feeling something in your bones, or a gut reaction. Each of these figures of speech expresses an understanding of the nature of intuition.

Sometimes intuition is thought to be a synonym (and a more acceptable term) for rudimentary ESP. "Women's intuition" may be a cliché that espresses that viewpoint.

The word intuition comes from a Latin root meaning to look at, to contemplate. These images suggest other images: to look within, to guard (as in to look at or watch), and knowledge or know (as in to look upon). We can see these various dimensions of the root meaning of intuition involved in the many forms of expression of intuition.

# THE NATURE OF INTUITION

In *The Intuitive Edge,* Philip Goldberg describes six types of intuition: discovery, generative, evaluative, operative, predictive, and illumination. Let's look at each one briefly.

*Discovery* intuition, or detection, provides insights into discoverable facts. It is the "Eureka!" phenomenon, made famous by Archimedes' experience in the bathtub. Stepping into the bathwater, he discovered that an object submerged in water displaces an amount of water equal to the volume of the object. The history of "serendipity" in science is full of accidental discoveries made possible by the intuitive recognition of the significance of an accidental observation. For example, noticing how coffee altered the color of a napkin led to the development of chromatography (analyzing substances by means of their color). Noticing how some photographic plates had been darkened led to the discovery of radioactivity. Other serendipitous discoveries include the development of Pap tests, how to culture skin for transplant to burn victims, radar, X-rays, Teflon, vulcanized rubber, penicillin, and aspartame.

*Generative* or creative intuition deals with opportunities, options, possibilities, and alternatives. Learning to be in the right place at the right time is one example. Artists and inventors experience this form of intuition as they ask, "I wonder what would happen if I tried this?" They have a vague inkling of the possibilities, even though later they might describe it as a happy accident.

*Evaluative* intuition is the inner voice that comments upon circumstances. Socrates is said to have remarked, "By the favor of the Gods, I have since my childhood been attended by a semidivine being whose voice from time to time dissuades me from some undertaking, but never directs me what I am to do." Cayce's technique for developing intuition begins with this inner voice.

*Operative* intuition guides our actions. Unlike evaluative intuition, it has nothing to evaluate, but is just an urge to do or not to do something. Vocational callings might be like this. One day during World War II, for no apparent reason, Winston Churchill suddenly decided not to enter his car in the usual way. Instead, he walked around to other side—and thus avoided injury from a bomb that exploded near the other side of the car.

*Predictive* intuition contains an element of prophesy— you are not necessarily moved to action, but you have a hunch that something will happen. For example, when you are driving, you may anticipate that another car is going to make a sudden move. I experience this intuition in my research work—being able to predict trends, anticipating ideas, or knowing the sort of information discovered today that will be relevant years later as a trend emerges.

*Illumination* is the greatest form of intuition. Mystical illumination transcends the other forms of intuition. Although illumination is the rarest form of intuition, Goldberg maintains that if it is developed, it will lead to the others. Like cosmic consciousness and related experiences, knower and known become one.

Cayce's approach to intuition is to be consistently guided by the highest form of any activity and try to find the reflection of the highest in the smallest form. His perspective is rooted in the concept of Oneness. He bases the nature of intuition on the inherent unity in creation.

From the axiomatic principle of Oneness, Cayce asserts the implication that all knowledge is within! Here he captures two of the meanings of the Latin root of the word intuition: inner and knowing, or knowing from within, consistent with the Taoist expression of the Perennial Philosophy, as articulated by Lao Tzu at the beginning of this chapter. For Cayce, intuition is not a phenomenon, but an ongoing reality that reflects our interconnectedness with life. The various forms of intuition can be explained as manifestations of this underlying Oneness.

We tend to think of intuition as an inferior, uncultivated form of ESP. While we might grant that some unrecognized psychic information lurks beneath a hunch, it seems inferior to an ESP experience, in which we have full conscious knowledge of the psychic information. Goldberg, however, maintains that intuition is not just an inferior form of ESP, but that it is more than ESP, in that it *goes beyond the information given*.

Cayce also felt that intuition was not an inferior or undeveloped form of ESP—he considered it to be ESP *plus*. On many occasions, when someone asked Cayce for a reading about developing psychic ability, Cayce's source indicated that it would be better to develop intuition than any other psychic ability. He called it the "higher development" of psychic ability. For him, intuition is the holistic intelligence (often speaking as the "still, small voice within") that puts together not just facts, but also possibilities, personal values, and need, to nudge you toward an opportunity, or to create a useful, practical, and concrete result. Whereas psychic ability might request, like Joe Friday, "Just the facts, ma'am," intuition searches out where-shall-I-go and what-shall-I-do with the perceived facts. Creativity and intuitive functioning are often linked in practice, because there is a creative aspect to intuition.

Suppose, for example, that I am struggling to understand a concept. I am standing in front of a bookcase. Perhaps one of the books may have something that could be helpful to me. Pure ESP could help me, to some extent. With clairvoyant ability I could, theoretically, touch the spine of each book and mentally scan its contents. Afterward, I could decide what might be helpful to me. Intuition, on the other hand, might direct me to a particular book. As I browse through the book "at random," I stumble on a passage that triggers an inspiration. ESP just gave me the facts, and I was left to sort them all out and decide what facts might be helpful. Intuition, on the other hand, led me right to what I needed.

In this example, intuition itself involved a creative act. It felt out a possibility, recognized its significance for helping me to get in touch with an idea that, as yet, did not exist in any of the books, but could be triggered in me—not in someone else—by a particular passage that

I stumbled onto "by chance." Synchronicities are often involved in intuition, demonstrating that intuition involves an attunement to a pattern of meaning. Thus intuition is a more holistic phenomenon than ESP, and more creative. Whereas psychic ability may yield information, intuition will usually yield results, decisions, calls to action, and other effects that have already been sorted through and evaluated as being in keeping with the needs, purposes, and values of the person.

## THE NEED-TO-KNOW BASIS OF INTUITIVE GUIDANCE

Cayce goes beyond these descriptive statements of intuition to give its purpose. Intuition plays a guiding role in our lives. It operates on a "need-to-know" basis. It is elicited by need, when we are in danger (as in the case of Winston Churchill), or when we are creatively striving for some goal. Intuition is purposeful, not random.

This purposeful quality of intuition is one of the reasons Cayce considers it to be the highest development of ESP. It provides no information that you do not need. In Cayce's biblical vernacular, intuition is higher than raw ESP because "knowledge not used is sin." We become responsible for knowledge that we obtain. Random ESP, or ESP performed out of curiosity, can burden us with information that we cannot use. Intuition doesn't burden us, but gives us only the information we need and prompts us in its use.

Archimedes' discovery is a good example of the need-to-know basis of intuition. What he discovered seems so obvious: push something into the water, and the water has to make as much room as the object takes up—its volume. Why hadn't anyone else noticed this relationship before? What enabled Archimedes to discover it? Archimedes had a need to know—he was working on an assaying problem, trying to determine the quality of gold in a crown. The principle he discovered helped solve his problem. Archimedes' need to know stimulated his intuition.

The need to know is a good basis for beginning to recognize and develop intuition. The way to prompt intuition is to create a situation where there is a strong *need* to know, but no apparent way of knowing. Intuition will go beyond the information given, so be sure to take the time to survey as many of the relevant facts as possible. This strategy forms the basis of Cayce's suggested experiment on learning to recognize intuition.

## LISTENING TO THE STILL, SMALL VOICE

How can we begin to recognize intuition? Cayce suggested starting with the simplest cases, where intuition can come into play in yes/no situations. They usually have to do with choices or decisions: Is this person telling me the truth? Would this be a good business investment? Is this really the career for me? Shall I take this job? Such decisions can be answered with a yes or a no.

Begin with some choice or decision that you have to make. Now use whatever resources you have that are relevant, and make your choice or decision. Study the situation, examine your feelings, make a list of pros and cons. This period of preparation is important. Intuitive information can build upon the foundation of information that you collect and evaluate at the conscious level. The period of preparation also places you into a position of attunement with the area or topic of your concern. After you have studied the situation, make your own decision.

Then go into a period of meditation. In the meditation, align your vibrations to the highest ideal, the most universal or encompassing pattern of truth, with the understanding that your decision is to be in harmony with that ideal. Then bring your decision into mind and ask yourself, "Is this the right choice?" Listen for your inner reaction. The inner prompting that you get, yes or no, is the act of intuition. It may come to you as a feeling, a thought, or you may even hear a voice saying, "No!" How your inner self will speak to you is something that you have to discover for yourself, but the response will come.

Cayce suggested this exercise specifically for learning to recognize the workings of intuition. It is also a workable form of seeking guidance. He suggests developing intuition by using it in an applied manner! If you will take real situations in which you care about the outcome, and apply yourself to figuring out a solution consciously, then seek a period of silence, you will experience an intuitive response to your choice or decision.

## FEELINGS AND IMAGES: COMMUNICATIONS FROM THE INNER SELF

Cayce's experiment requires responding to one's inner self. Intuition, and its still, small voice, may come in a variety of guises, including feelings and images. Feelings, and imagery especially, can be the manifestation of the inner voice providing intuitive information. Remember Hans Jenny's vibratory patterns? When we are concerned about a particular topic or situation, we become attuned to it—our being begins to resonate to the vibrations of the situation. Our inner self begins to manifest the effects of that resonance by producing analogous patterns of its own, in the form of feelings and images.

Albert Einstein gave free rein to his imagination. Pondering the nature of time, he imagined being a clock that was hurled through space, traveling faster and faster. That image led him to the development of his relativity theory. Another famous example in the history of science was Kekula's discovery of the formula of the benzene ring. Pondering the nature of organic compounds, he found himself imagining a snake curled back on itself, biting its tail. He recognized in that image the pattern for the formula he was seeking. In such cases of scientific discoveries, the seekers were so intently involved with the problem at hand that they unconsciously became "one with" the object of study. Their whole being—their thinking, their feelings and imagination, their actions and their attention—became attuned to the vibrations of the mystery. This created a resonance between them and what they wanted to discover. The intuitive breakthrough was a manifestation of this attunement.

I am reminded of detectives who declare that in order to catch a criminal, you have to think like one. They express the resonance theme of intuitive discovery. By imaginatively becoming attuned to the mind of the criminal, the criminal is ultimately revealed to them. The Native American communicates with inanimate objects in nature in a similar way: to learn the wisdom of a particular stone, attune yourself to the stone. Open yourself up meditatively and allow the stone's vibrations to become your own. The Native American respects the flow of imagery in the imagination as a source of revelation, not a fantasy. As I meditate on the stone, according to the Native American approach, the stone's message will come to me through the imagination. As I contemplate the stone, my thoughts, feelings, and imagery are assumed to be the effect of the stone's vibrations upon me.

When I am in a counseling situation, listening deeply to a person's story, I find that I pay little attention to the words, and concentrate more on the sound of the person's voice. The music of the voice is giving expression to what is going on at deeper levels within the person. The soul sings or cries through the sound of the voice. As I allow myself to listen in this way, it is almost as if I become hypnotized by the sound of the person's voice, becoming one with its tones and vibrations. As I do so, my body seems to resonate to the sound of that voice, my being resonates with the being of the person, and I can feel it. As I focus on these feelings, images and scenes appear in my mind. I have learned that these spontaneous fantasies, far from being a sign of not paying attention, are manifestations of intuitive knowledge about the person.

When I share these images and fantasies with the person, I discover their meaningfulness. The images are usually not literally true. Their symbolic form is another aspect of the patterning of vibrations. Symbolic images are often highly condensed patterns of information. Just as we say "a picture is worth a thousand words," a symbolic image may contain several juxtaposed images, combining information in a creative way that reveals a hidden truth. Dreams, the image factory *par excellence,* are thus a valuable source of symbolic intuitions.

## INTUITION AS OPEN CHANNELING

Listening to the still, small voice within is a form of channeling. We say intuition involves knowing something without knowing how we know it. Have you ever had the experience of making a statement with conviction, then wondering afterward, as you marveled at the truth of what you said, "How did I know that?" We could we say you were channeling—channeling information intuitively. In *Channeling: The Intuitive Connection,* William Kautz and Melanie Branon define channeling as a form of intuition, as an "inner process, an intuitive connection with a universal but unseen source of information and insight." John Klimo, in *Channeling: Investigations on Receiving Information from Paranormal Sources,* calls intuition "open channeling." He includes inspiration and creativity as other forms of open channeling, which he defines as "the ability to act as a vehicle for thoughts, images, feelings, and information coming from a source that is beyond the individual's self and from beyond ordinary reality (as we know it)—a source that is not identifiable and does not identify itself."

Cayce would call this channeling the "higher Self," the soul-self that is in touch with the universal consciousness. Cayce's trance state could be considered an example of open channeling developed to the state of universal clairvoyance.

Like other forms of intuition, the open channeling we call intuition often occurs in response to a need. As a speaker—and I've heard similar stories from other speakers—I sometimes digress from my planned remarks and launch into an impromptu commentary. While my mouth is churning out this material, I often marvel at the source of the ideas ("Hey! that's pretty good stuff!" I may think to myself). After the talk, someone invariably approaches me and says they weren't sure why they came to the lecture, but my spontaneous remarks about so and so answered a real need. Open channeling can have a psychic component as well!

Often open channeling is prompted by a question. In lecturing, I have found that the question-and-answer session at the end often involves instances of inspired speech. A person's question, and the feelings that I sense behind the question, often trigger an intuitive response. It was said of Cayce that when he went into his trance, if he wasn't asked a question promptly he would go to sleep! I myself have felt that the energy of the question often is the source of inspiration for the answer. Cayce maintained that the desire of the questioner determined the type of material that came through his trance channel. It reminds me of how often I have heard that deciding on the most appropriate question is often most of the battle in getting the most helpful answer.

## CHANNELING INTUITION: INSPIRATIONAL WRITING

Cayce gave a form for people to experience open channeling. It is an extension of the first exercise, learning to listen to the still, small voice. The first exercise Cayce gave has two uses. First, it is useful to get acquainted with the intuitional "force" within, and how it appears or feels to you. The second use is for using intuition to comment on a decision or choice. For more open-ended situations, where you desire something beyond a simple yes/no answer, Cayce suggested a different kind of experiment: inspirational writing.

Helen Cohn Schucman channeled *A Course in Miracles* through a process of inspirational writing. It began with the experience of an inner voice. She had experienced other inner events, so she was already sensitive to inner promptings. She wrote a few lines at first, then stopped. She had a hard time accepting the phenomenon. But the inner promptings did not stop. She described the process as like taking dictation. She was not in a trance, it was not automatic writing. Robert Skutch's *Journey Without Distance,* about this inspired text, shows what can be accomplished through inspirational writing.

Learning to listen to the yes/no response of the inner voice would certainly be a good way to practice before attempting inspirational writing, for in this approach to channeling, more than simply yes or no will be expressed. After you feel comfortable responding to the inner self, you might attempt some inspirational writing.

The easiest way to understand this form of open channeling is by observing your breathing and how it operates and interacts with your awareness of it. Most of the time we pay no attention to our breathing. It is automatic. Now, for a moment, pay attention to it. When you first notice your breathing, you have the sensation that your are controlling your breath, the timing of inhalation and exhalation. Try to relax, then in a moment gently observe your breathing and see if you can observe it without controlling it.

If you relax, and are patient enough, you will gradually begin to witness your breathing as it happens all by itself, the way it happens all the time on its own when you are not paying any attention to it. Observing your breathing without interfering with it is an ancient form of meditation. If you practice it, you will find that during the exhalation, you let go and become very relaxed, and during the inhalation, you witness the mystery of *inspiration!* That the word *inspire* is used to describe the intake of breathing may give you a clue about *inspiration* as it is used in creativity. The processes are related.

Now let's consider three forms of writing. The first is *conscious, intentional writing.* This is what we all do on our first attempt, as with the first attempt at observing our breath. We feel we are in control, that we have to think up what to write, and we are conscious of our choice of words or of our lack of words to express what is on our mind. We sit back and try to think up something to write, and then write it down. That is intentional writing.

Another form is *automatic writing.* Just as we can breathe automatically without paying any attention to the process, it is possible for some people to write without paying any attention to their writing. By distracting, blocking, or blanking the mind, they have learned to let the "unconscious speak directly" through their writing. The writer is unconscious of what is being written. At the time of writing, the person is in some form of dissociated state, distracted or in trance. Automatic writing is one form of channeling entities, disincarnate spirits, or multiple personalities. It is a form of channeling that Cayce, and others familiar with its hazards, often warned about using. In automatic breathing, when we become upset, our breath responds accordingly. Sometimes we breathe fast, and sometimes we actually stop breathing, or hold back the breath—the breath expresses the problem or upset. In the same way, automatic writing can express the discord, fear, and groping in a person's life. Or it can express power strivings, struggles to achieve, to "get on top" or to "get one's way." It can be seductive. It doesn't necessarily express the best, nor is it the most creative.

The third form, *inspirational writing,* is like observing your breathing without interfering with it. With inspirational writing, you are aware of the purpose of the writing, and you are aware of what you write as you write it, but you experience the writing as almost happening by itself.

To perform inspirational writing, you reverse the usual procedure. Normally, as in conscious, intentional writing, you first think up what you want to say, then you record your thoughts. In inspirational writing, you do the reverse: you begin by writing, with your purpose in mind, and you observe what you write. You are not recording your thoughts on paper, but rather you are noting in awareness what you write.

To prepare for inspirational writing, it helps to focus on your breathing for a moment, reminding yourself that you can be aware of your breathing without stopping the flow, before you begin each writing exercise. Before you begin, it is important to meditate. In meditation, we try to quiet the mind and tune into our highest thoughts. Highest means the most universal perspective. With meditation comes a sense of peace and of being at one with life. Often, if questions are posed, a very different sort of answer is given. Meditation itself is a form of channeling—channeling the creative forces throughout our body.

Cayce suggests setting an atmosphere conducive to inspirational writing: dim lighting, perhaps some quiet music. Incense may be appropriate, if it reminds you of an elevated state of consciousness. Then set your pen to paper. Following the ideas we have set forth about intuition operating on a need-to-know basis, it is better to choose a topic that concerns you deeply. If you will listen or accept what is there, the ideas will emerge for you to set down on paper. Simply begin to write, noting what is being written; don't wait for an experience of being dictated to.

Journal writing has recently become popular as a form of gaining inspiration and using intuition. As a result, other inspirational methods have been developed. Ira Progoff, in developing his *Intensive Journal* method, for example, suggests writing a dialogue between yourself and your higher Self. You pose the questions and your higher Self answers them. I have found that people often get very good information this way, but it is important to ask follow-up questions and not simply accept high-minded statements at face value. For example, perhaps your higher Self writes, "Be at peace with yourself." You recognize this as good advice, and may be tempted to accept it as given. Later, however, you realize that you don't know how to be at peace with yourself. So you ask a follow-up question: "How can I be at peace with myself?" Then your higher Self will answer in more detail.

Cayce advised not to look upon inspirational writing as a phenomenal object of curiosity, although it may be. Instead, try to take something from the writing and put it into practice. If you act on the guidance given, testing out the ideas, you will form a stronger link with your source of intuition. The next time you attempt to do inspirational writing to channel intuition, the information will be noticeably better.

## INTUITION IN BUSINESS

It's the "imagineers versus the engineers" in the business of the future, says Weston Agor, a political scientist and psychologist who consults for business training intuition. He is the author of the best-selling book *Intuitive Management.* Business is quick to adopt something that works, and intuition is big business to those who can teach it. Businesspeople have always used their intuition, and many even knew that they were doing so; but most have not recognized it as such or have kept it a secret. Now, however, intuition is coming out of the closet.

Several years ago Douglas Dean, of the Newark College of Engineering, tested his theory that capable managers are probably good at ESP. His *Executive ESP* is full of stories of business hunches that paid off in a big way. Many businesspeople had mentioned the use of intuition in preparing sealed bids. Besides evaluating all the known facts and information, they used their hunches about how the numbers would come out in the bids. Dean bet that ESP played a role in intuitive decisions, so he tested managers with a special ESP game that involved predicting the future.

Dean devised an experiment that was almost like a lottery. He asked the managers to guess a one hundred digit number that a computer would generate later through a random process. The type of ESP required was precognition. After the managers' guesses had been made, the computer generated the number series, and the managers' scores were tabulated. Dean tested hundreds of managers and also maintained profiles of them. He found that those managers who were responsible for companies that made good profits were significantly more accurate in their ESP prognostications than were the less successful managers. His work provided evidence for the role of ESP in the intuitive business decisions of executives and was a primary instigator in the development of the current interest in business intuition.

Edgar Cayce was often asked business questions, and many businesspeople asked him about their use of intuition and psychic ability in business affairs. His advice was to adopt a holistic approach. He emphasized the importance of founding a business on a high ideal. Trying to develop a good product that would serve people well is a prime example of such an ideal, and it also makes good sense in business. He promised that a business that was sincerely founded on such a spiritual ideal would be a natural for success. He once indicated that AT&T, for example, because of its original ideal of helping people to communicate, would have a hard time failing, in spite of poor business practices.

The second aspect of Cayce's advice was for the businessperson to combine the study of the facts of the business with self-study, and the study of spiritual laws. He indicated that the businessperson would find that the patterns in the business and the patterns in the person's life overlapped. And they reflected the patterns of spiritual truths. In such a context, the businessperson could expect to receive intuitive and psychic guidance concerning the business. Cayce approached intuition holistically as a creative expression of the whole person, not simply a special, single "muscle" to be used from time to time.

I have found that true in my own work, as well as in training people in creativity. I ask them to focus on a specific dilemma in their work, and try to do their best. Their obstacles at work also reflect their own internal problems, as well as universal patterns concerning life's difficulties. Although it is commonly assumed that one should keep one's personal and professional lives separate, the separation is artificial and cuts a person off from sources of inspiration in both areas.

I once worked with one artist, a ceramic designer who

was dissatisfied with the textures she was able to produce on dinnerware. We spent a lot of time talking about what bowls and plates meant to her. She had her private meanings, which she didn't think were particularly relevant, as well as her public, professional rationale concerning dishes. She then had a dream about a shrimp boat. Discussion of that dream revealed a worry that she would "miss the boat," a concern she had about her life in general as well as about her art, a fear that she didn't have what it takes, or that she had the "wrong stuff" and would get left behind. I had the impression that she had the "right stuff," but was sitting on it because it didn't match what she thought was expected and professionally appropriate, or because it wouldn't gain her the recognition she sought. She was approaching her work left-handed, as it were, since she kept her better hand behind her back—her genuine, inner Self. When she got to talking about shrimp, I noticed that although she said she didn't like them, she was able to describe their texture in some detail. It seemed as if she resonated deeply to the texture of shrimp shells, so I suggested that she explore this texture in her ceramics. Out of this exploration came a new textural vocabulary, which she developed in her work. As part of this artistic breakthrough also came more self-acceptance and confidence concerning the value of her own inclinations. The professional and personal dimensions grew simultaneously.

Confidence to be yourself in your work seems to be an important ingredient in creativity and intuitive functioning in one's business. Here is another dimension of the holistic nature of intuition: it is the quality of the person that determines creativity, intuition, and psychic awareness.

## INTUITION, CREATIVITY, AND PSYCHIC AWARENESS: THE PERSONAL PATTERN

Cayce maintained that intuition is an inner response and the intuitive person is one who is familiar with the inner Self. Intuition is an expression of the whole person; it is not just a simple technique or an isolated skill. This is Cayce's holistic viewpoint, and the evidence seems to be in Cayce's favor. The personality profile of the intuitive person matches the profile for creativity and psychic ability, just as Cayce had maintained. Let's look at how researchers have identified that profile.

An experiment that has proved highly influential in the history of personality tests and research requires one to respond on the basis of an inner feeling. It is called the "rod and frame" test. Imagine this situation: You are seated in a chair in a darkened room. On the other side of the room hangs an illuminated rod, a smooth, straight stick. The rod is hanging fairly straight up and down, but it can be rotated slightly by a control knob that you have in your hand. Your task is to turn the knob back and forth until the rod is straight up and down, along a true vertical. The test doesn't measure eyesight, but whether you can determine, from your inner sense, when the rod is vertical. To do that, you have to align yourself inwardly with gravity and with the rod and make a comparison between the rod's position and your sense of the vertical. People vary in their ability to make a correct determination of the vertical.

The real test comes when a frame is placed around the rod. The frame is purposely put a bit off the vertical, and then you have to determine the verticality of the rod. It is easy to be misled by the frame. Solving the test requires ignoring what your outer-directed senses are telling you in favor of cues you are getting from your body. You need your outer-directed senses to examine the verticality of the rod, but you have to ignore what your senses are telling you about the frame. The measure of verticality has to come from within.

People who can determine true verticality from this test are called "field independent," because they can operate independently of the external field created by the frame. This experimental testing procedure has been used to good effect to predict such personality traits as creativity, openness to inner experience, dream recall, and other aspects of intuition. It is a good example to show very concretely what it means to be in touch with one's "inner" self.

A similar pattern of traits has been found among intuitive people. Malcolm Westcott, in *Toward a Contemporary Psychology of Intuition,* described his extensive research on a particular type of intuition, the ability to perceive patterns. For example, in the number series 1, 2, 1, 2 . . . what comes next? Easy, it's 1. What about this series: 1, 4, 5, 2 . . . what comes next? Not so easy. What if I show some more of it: 1, 4, 5, 2, 5, 6, 3, 6, 7 . . . what comes next? The answer is 4 (the series is made of triplets; 4, 7, 8 comes up next). Westcott presented such number series and determined how many numbers the person needed to see before being willing to make a guess, and how accurate the guess was. The number series were based on patterns, not complicated mathematical configurations. He felt that it was a fair measure of intuition in that it asked a person to attempt to go beyond the information given and detect a pattern. The role of ESP could not be ruled out in his tests, although he did not consider that factor in his treatment of intuition. He also gave the people extensive personality testing, to see what traits corresponded with this type of intuitive ability.

The intuitive person needed little information and formed the correct guess. Westcott found these people to be creative, confident and self-sufficient, independent and spontaneous. They based their identity on personal and inner factors rather than on membership in any group or class. They were resistant to outside control, willing to risk criticism, and capable of handling doubt and uncertainty. They tended to be a bit unconventional, and were comfortable with it. And they scored high on field independence, that trait measured by tests such as the rod and frame experiment.

Parapsychologists have found that creativity tests can predict performance in ESP situations. For example, Gertrude Schmeidler tested students' ability to predict the sequence of patterns that a computer would generate through a random process. She also tested them on various creativity tasks, such as thinking of different uses for a brick. She found that the students who exhibited the most ESP also scored the highest in creativity.

## MEDITATION AND THE DEVELOPMENT OF THE INTUITIVE PERSONALITY

Meditation seems to be the best all-around approach to developing the personal pattern that highly intuitive people display. The pattern, manifesting as intuition, creativity, and psychic ability, is composed of such traits as field independence, openness and trust in one's inner experience, spontaneity, self-confidence, tolerance of ambiguity and doubt, and a willingness to risk criticism, to name but a few of the attributes of the inner-directed person. This profile fits with Cayce's assertion that intuition comes from within. It might seem that to develop all these traits a complete personality makeover would be required. But a personality change is not what is needed; it is learning to look and know what is within.

To develop a personal profile conducive to intuition it is not necessary to see a psychologist. In *Focusing*, Eugene Gendlin discusses the ability to look within, and describes processes for doing so. In his research, he has found that psychotherapy is effective only to the extent that it trains this ability. He has found, as have many others, that the very act of learning how to focus on inner events, feelings, and images is itself therapeutic. So perhaps there is a more direct route to developing the various personality traits that support intuition. Cayce and others who have studied intuition seem to agree that meditation is the best training and preparation for the development of the intuitive personality. Meditation certainly is a process of turning within!

Meditation can help us develop aspects of the intuitive profile. For example, meditation has been found to increase field independence. This effect makes sense, for through meditation a person becomes more sensitive and familiar with inner sensations and signals.

We become relaxed while in meditation, so the sensations, feelings, and other signals are less disturbing. It is easier to allow them to come along and pass by. Meditation researcher Daniel Goleman theorized that meditation is like a generic form of psychotherapy, because while we meditate, we come to accept without distress whatever arises. We develop openness and self-acceptance during meditation. A recent study of meditation and psychotherapy conducted by Herbert Benson, M.D., of Harvard University confirmed this theory. He found that meditators had various experiences during meditation that speeded up the process of therapy: childhood memories, new insights, release of suppressed emotions. Such events help us become more comfortable with our inner Self, more tolerant of its expressions.

Knowing what your feelings are, knowing when you are having them, being able to detect them, being able to identify them, respecting them—these traits are part of the package of self-acceptance that comes from personal growth, whether through therapy, meditation, or the school of life experience. Intuition depends on them, for it is necessary to be in touch with feelings to recognize intuition. Accepting feelings even when they don't correspond with one's thoughts and reasoning is part of acknowledging intuition. All these components of the profile of the intuitive personality can be developed through meditation. It is available to you at any moment. It is as easy as breathing—the inspiration of the energy that links us with all life.

# 5
# DREAMS: THE PSYCHIC DOORWAY

*The dream is a little hidden door in the innermost
and most secret recesses of the soul, opening into
that cosmic night which was psyche long before
there was any ego-consciousness.*

CARL JUNG

*In sleep the soul seeks the real diversion or the real
activity of self. Those who are nearer the spiritual
realm more often retain their visions and dreams
on awakening.*

EDGAR CAYCE reading no. 5754–3

THE CHANCES ARE EXCELLENT that a dream
will provide your first psychic experience. My own interest in dreams was first inspired by this realization. I had
a gifted artist friend, Jim Turrell, who was "into Cayce"
and used his dreams as a "guide." I had heard of using
dreams only in the context of psychotherapy. Jim's
dreams excited him and gave an added dimension to his
life. One day, he drove me to his new studio near the
beach in Santa Monica. I was surprised when he said
that he found this low-rent, spacious, and enviably situ-
ated place through a dream. His dead father, he confided, had appeared to him in a dream, pointed out a
building with its large windows painted over, and told
him that it would make an excellent studio. Upon awakening, my friend drove around until he found the build-

ing he had seen in his dream. It was just what he wanted.

On another occasion, Jim came by after a long absence and told me he had had a dream in which a mutual friend of ours was in serious trouble. He decided to make the long trip to see our friend and check it out. The dream had proved accurate, and he was able to help. I was impressed, not just by his dreaming ability and his confidence in his dreams, which I had come to expect, but by his willingness to extend himself for a friend. It was all part of what he called "the Cayce trip": attunement and service.

Jim's life was exciting, and the idea of using dreams as a guide appealed to me. But I had not recalled a dream since childhood. At his suggestion, I made a resolution to keep a dream diary, and thus began a new relationship with dreams. I put the diary by my bed, and went to sleep with the notion that the next day would be the first day of my new life. The next day came, but no dreams came along. So did the next, and the next, and still no dreams. In fact, the first day of my new life didn't come along for three months! That's how long it took for my diary to sit by my bedside unused before I finally awakened with a dream.

It was another four months before I had my second dream. My third dream didn't occur until about a year after I made my diary. But that first dream turned out to be one of the most significant of my life, for it initiated me into the spiritual process of recovery from alcoholism. As Charles Whitfield, M.D., explains in *Alcoholism and Spirituality,* it is an approach that is now popular today in the field of New Age therapy. Although I didn't realize it until several years later, this dream proved to be prophetic also about the type of dream research studies that I would later conduct. I wrote *Getting Help from Your Dreams* about that research, from all that I learned as a result of having had so much trouble remembering and interpreting my dreams.

# THE MOST COMMON SOURCE OF PSYCHIC EXPERIENCES

The most common—and one of the most useful—forms of psychic ability that you can develop is in your dreams. That dreams can contain psychic information may come as no surprise to you. Chances are that if you have had any experience at all that makes you believe in the reality of psychic awareness, it came to you in a dream. Louisa E. Rhine (wife of J. B. Rhine and cofounder with her husband of the first parapsychology laboratory in the country, at Duke University) tells stories from all over the world about psychic experiences, most of them involving dreams, in *Hidden Channels of the Mind.* Researchers at the University of Virginia, after surveying college students and local inhabitants of surrounding Charlottesville, found that the majority of reported psychic experiences involved dreams. In reviewing research into over 9,300 cases of documented psychic experiences, Ian Stevenson calculated that 57 percent of them happened in dreams. In *Telepathic Impressions,* Dr. Stevenson concluded that dreams are the primary psychic doorway.

You have probably already had several psychic experiences in dreams without realizing it. Cayce was asked to interpret hundreds of dreams, and many times he pointed out psychic information in the dream. In many of these interpretations, as well as in documented cases from other sources, the person had no idea that the dream had a psychic source. Sometimes the dream seemed ordinary, other times not so ordinary, but the idea of its being psychic did not occur to the person until a later discovery proved it to be so. Chances are excellent that if you could produce a record of all the dreams you have ever had, remembered or not, your own examination of these dreams would convince you that you have already had several psychic experiences.

# PSYCHIC DREAMING IN THE LABORATORY

One of the most convincing laboratory experiments demonstrating the reality of ESP in dreams was conducted at Maimonides Hospital in Brooklyn. A complete account of this work is given in *Dream Telepathy,* by Montague Ullman, M.D., and Stanley Krippner, Ph.D., the principal investigators. Their simple procedure is worth describing, for others have adapted it to perform their own experiments, as you may wish to do.

If you were a participant in one of the experiments at Maimonides, you'd sleep in the laboratory, wired to electronic monitors used to determine when you were dreaming. In a different room, a person acting as your "agent" would stay awake all night and focus on a randomly selected piece of artwork, trying to send the images in the picture to your dreaming mind. The agent would examine the artwork, think about it, practice visualizing the picture in detail, recall personal memories that the picture evoked, imagine being in the picture, interacting with the scene, and otherwise become personally involved with the picture, in the hopes of charging the ESP message with emotion. Whenever the electronic monitors indicated that you were dreaming, an experimenter would awaken you to collect your dream report. The next day, both you and independent judges would be shown a group of art prints, and asked to identify the one used by the agent based upon the dream reports you provided the night before.

For example, in one experiment the target picture was Marc Chagall's *Paris from a Window,* which shows a man observing the colorful Paris skyline. The picture has several distinctive elements—a cat with a human face, several men flying in the air, and a chair sprouting flowers. Here are some of the excerpts from the five dream reports obtained that night: "bees flying around flowers . . . I was walking. For some reason, I say French Quarter . . . talking with a group of Shriners. . . . They had on a hat that looked more like a French policeman's hat . . . some sort of romantic type of architecture—buildings, village, quaint . . . a man walking through one of these villages, these towns. It would definitely be in the nineteenth century. . . . French attire . . . walking up the side of a hill above the other layers of the town . . . it's a festive thing . . . the Mardi Gras type."

Clearly, the dreams reflected the contents of the picture. Note, however, that the dreams are merely *influenced* by the picture; they are not distinctly *about* the picture or about the person trying to "send" the picture. If the dreamer had a dream like that outside the ESP laboratory, it is doubtful he would have recognized it as telepathic. He probably would have regarded it as ordinary, never suspecting that it was the result of telepathy. Even in many of these experiments, the dreamer does not recognize the resemblance between the picture and the dreams, while the judges can clearly see the connection. Chances are that you have had several dreams that were the result of telepathy, and were never the wiser.

## DREAMING OF THE FUTURE

Cayce claimed that nothing of significance ever happened in our lives without our dreaming of it first. Perhaps dreaming of future events—precognitive dreaming—seems more far-fetched to you than telepathic dreaming, yet surveys have revealed that dreams about the future are much more common than telepathic dreams. One survey, reported in the March 1978 issue of *Psychology Today* by psychologist David Ryback, indicated that 8 percent of the population—or nearly 2 million Americans—has had a dream that "came true." Perhaps it is because dreams about the future have a greater chance of being discovered, while many telepathic dreams remain undetected.

The Maimonides group was able to demonstrate precognitive dreaming in the laboratory. Malcolm Bessent, a psychic who had a history of being able to predict the future, volunteered for the study. The Maimonides method was changed in important ways to test for Bessent's precognitive ability. The art prints that had served as the targets in the telepathy studies were elaborated into multisensory experiences. The plan was that *after* Bessent slept in the lab and had his dreams, a scenario would be selected at random, and Bessent would be exposed to an experience based on that scenario. Bessent's task was to dream of the experience *before it had even been chosen.*

On one night, some of Bessent's dreams included the following: ". . . impression of green and purple . . . small areas of white and blue"; ". . . a building . . . a patient . . . a white coat like a doctor's coat"; "hostility toward me by people in a group I was in daily contact with . . . they were doctors and medical people"; "drinking . . . eating."

The next morning, an experimenter who knew nothing of Bessent's dreams randomly selected a scenario. It turned out to be one based on Van Gogh's *Hospital Corridor at St. Remy,* which portrays a patient in the hallway of a mental hospital. The colors in the painting are orange, green, deep blue, and white. The experiential scenario designed around this picture was then carried out on Bessent: music from Rosza's "Spellbound" was played, and he was addressed as Mr. Van Gogh by the experimenter, who was dressed in a white coat. He was then shown several slides of mental patients. He himself was treated like a patient, given a pill and a glass of water. He was "disinfected" with acetone daubed on him with a cotton swab, then led through a darkened hallway out of the laboratory to the experimenter's office. Bessent knew the experimenter personally, and found it strange to be treated this way, even though he knew it was part of the experiment. He sensed a definite subjective connection between his dream and the experiences he was led through the next morning.

Independent judges agreed. When given a transcript of the dreams, and eight different art pictures and associated experiential scenarios to evaluate, they unanimously chose the "corridor" experience as most closely matching Bessent's dreams. In all, Bessent spent sixteen nights in the lab trying to dream precognitively of the scenario that would be selected for him the next morning. On fourteen of these sixteen experiments, the judges correctly matched Bessent's dreams with the scenario that was chosen the following morning.

## THE CREATIVE ENIGMA OF THE DREAM

Decades before this research, Edgar Cayce advised that dreams were the most readily available avenue to psychic awareness. He encouraged people to recall their dreams, to study them. He indicated that any aspect of ESP, any "reality" encountered in an altered state of consciousness, or any other "mystery" of the mind, including death, could be experienced and explored in dreams. He also indicated that dreams were the safest way to explore these regions. In making this claim, Cayce was speaking out of an ancient tradition. Nothing in the history of human experience has had such a profound impact on culture as the dream.

In *Our Dreaming Mind: History and Psychology,* Robert Van de Castle describes dreams that led to the world's religions, including Buddhism, Mohammedism, and Christianity, as well as dreams that resulted in scientific discoveries, inventions, and works of art. He also describes dreams that played a role in world history and shaped political careers, led to the recovery of lost objects or treasures, or offered advice on the stock market. Dreams have also been an inspiration and an enigma to philosophers.

But what is a dream? What happens when we dream? The nocturnal experience seems real, and yet it did not actually happen. If the dream is real, it is some other kind of reality. Some have called it a vision in the night, suggesting that the experience was real, but on a different plane of reality. Others have called it a trip the soul makes, to account for the presence of faraway scenes. Each explanation is an attempt to account for the apparent reality of the dream. Edgar Cayce incorporated both views into his explanation.

# FALLING ASLEEP:
# DAWN OF PSYCHIC AWARENESS

One way to develop psychic awareness, suggested Cayce, is to be more observant of the process of falling asleep. Cayce explains that as we go to sleep our sensitivity changes to a different level of vibration, a different frequency. In the sleeping state, our psychic self emerges. It is rather like the stars—they are always there, but we can't see them in the daytime because the sun is too bright.

Cayce called sleep the "shadow" of death. He said it was like death in two respects: first, because consciousness becomes unaware of physical conditions surrounding the body; and second, because there awakens a larger awareness that transcends time and space, an awareness available after death. Cayce described the awakening of the "sixth sense" in sleep as occurring through a similar process. Why not try to stay awake and meet it?

When falling asleep, Cayce points out, we become less aware in the normal sense. The mind of the physical body, the cerebral-spinal system of muscles and sensory impressions, is shutting down. You may have experienced this shutting down, for example, when drifting off to sleep in front of the TV, or when someone was reading aloud. Suddenly, you realize that you haven't been hearing what was going on but were in a world of your own. Your conscious mind was going to sleep, and you were awakening to your subconscious mind.

Cayce qualifies his statement about the senses shutting down by pointing out that they remain alert to the extent necessary to remain on guard for the protection of the sleeping person. He says that it is as if we keep "an ear cocked," in case some event should require us to awaken and take action. It's likely that you suddenly woke up to the TV set or to the person reading because you heard something of special importance.

While consciousness is shutting down its response to most physical information, it is simultaneously opening up to information from the imagination of the subconscious mind. Falling asleep may be defined as reversing the usual situation: the outside becomes unconscious, and the subconscious becomes conscious. We exchange waking reality for dreaming reality. Here is the shift of vibration that corresponds with falling asleep: our vibrational pattern shifts and we tune to a different spectrum of reality. That we are still aware of our imagination and of unconscious processes is another aspect of Cayce's assertion that sleep is like death, for in both states we interact with these dimensions. It is not surprising, then, that Cayce was sometimes asked by people about strange experiences that occur upon falling asleep. Hearing voices, unusual changes in the perception of the body, and such are commonplace in that twilight zone.

As we continue to fall asleep, according to Cayce, our senses undergo a change. Hearing, for example, becomes activated throughout the body. "Listen to what your body is trying to tell you." Have you ever heard that advice? It is a suggestion to pay attention to subtle clues from your body. The subconscious mind does just that during sleep. It operates not just through the brain, but through the lymph centers and the sympathetic nervous system. That is why we often have dreams about the condition of the body that warn us of possible health problems before they are diagnosed by a physician. In *The Dream Worlds of Pregnancy,* Eileen Stukane describes how women commonly dream of the development of the fetus during pregnancy.

Such awareness during sleep, Cayce would have us imagine, is like "listening" with the "third ear." He calls the awareness that awakens in us as we fall asleep the "sixth sense." It is a form of ESP. As our awareness diffuses throughout the body, we awaken to our psychic awareness. Dreams are one of the experiences of this sixth sense!

# WHAT IS A DREAM?

Cayce likens the process of dreaming to the mythical
and biblical theme of death and resurrection. When
Jesus died in the body, he was reborn in a spirit form.
Similarly, in the process of falling asleep, we die to our
physical existence but awaken to our spiritual reality.
Cayce indicates that the dreamer is the soul. When we
fall asleep, our soul awakens. A dream is an experience
of the soul.

What does the soul do when it dreams? The soul has
universal awareness, which includes its memories from
its experiences in past lives, particularly lessons learned.
The soul, possessing the wisdom of multilife experience,
brings that perspective to bear as it reviews events and
experiences of the previous day. This evaluation of a
day's life from the overall perspective of several lifetimes is somewhat like the judgment parents make
about events in the life of their child. The child's own
values may appear particularly ironic, poignant, humor-
ous, sad, or hopeful when viewed from the wider perspective of the adult.

# THE PURPOSE OF DREAMING

The purpose of dreams is guidance. Just as a parent
evaluates the behavior of the child from an adult perspective, the soul examines the person's experiences
from the viewpoint of lifetimes of learning. It is this
experience of evaluation that is the dream, and the purpose of the dream. It is one of the main ways the soul
has of guiding the person. How we are doing, what we
are doing, where we are headed is compared with where
we really want to go, how we really want to be. Dreams
are experiences of discovery—"Ah-ha!"—when we see
from the soul's point of view what our daily experiences
mean to us. You might say it is the comparison of ideals
with reality.

How does this guidance function? Cayce again uses
one of the attunement words. He says that the soul's

experience (or evaluative perception) during the dream resonates with us after we awaken. The dream content we recall is what we are able to remember of the soul's experience. For the soul, it was a discovery experience, but we recall it as a story with strange symbols. Even if we do not understand the symbols, or even if we do not recall the dream, we are left with the effects of the soul's experience resonating within us when we awaken. Sometimes we awaken in a particular mood that is a carryover of a dream, an echo of the soul's experience. The soul, having formed over many lifetimes an ideal such as love or peace, compares that ideal with the previous day's activities as we sleep. It can ache, mourn, or wish that our daily experience would profit by what was learned in the past. Those feelings, the aching or mourning, carry over into our mood the next day, shaping our emotions and behavior. In this way the soul, through its dreams, offers to guide us.

Cayce's view of the function of dreams resembles several currently popular theories of dreaming. First, it is almost universally accepted that dreams are necessary to our survival, that we have a need to dream. Theorists differ on what happens in a dream that is so important. Many have adopted the view that dreams are the brain's way of sorting through the day's memories and organizing them for long-term storage, putting recent memories into the context of a lifetime of learning. Experiments have shown, for example, that a person who is prevented from dreaming is likely to have a poorer memory of the previous day's events. A good book that represents this point of view is *Landscapes of the Night,* by Christopher Evans. His computer-processing theory parallels Cayce's view; both argue that dreams are a way to review the day's experience in terms of past experience. Evans asserts that the brain reviews the day's events in the manner of a computer; Cayce claims the soul does the reviewing, scanning memories from more than this one life.

Carl Jung's theory of dreams fits nicely between modern computer theories and Cayce. Jung also believed that the purpose of dreaming was for guidance. Jung was not averse to referring to the soul as the source of guidance, for he believed he had found evidence that during dreams the mind is able to scan information that lies beyond the time and space constraints of the person's own lifetime. Jung envisioned the guidance operating through a process he called "compensation." In his view, a dream provided a compensatory experience, something that would balance out the experiences of the day to make a more rounded total experience. His theory of guidance is thus much like Cayce's, as he too found that the dream experience itself often accomplished the purpose of the dream. Jung believed that dream interpretation was something the conscious person could do in order to have a better appreciation for the movements within, but was not necessary to accomplish those movements. It was better, he felt, to be able to work with the dream, because then you could participate and cooperate with the movement the dream had initiated.

We do not have to interpret dreams in order for them to do their job. This makes sense—we recall so few of our dreams, and understand fewer of them. If the dream were dependent on our being able to recall and understand it in order for it to fulfill its purpose, we would be in a sorry state.

## REMEMBERING DREAMS

If you have trouble remembering your dreams, you are not alone. Estimates have suggested that perhaps as much as 90 percent of the dream life of the total population is never recalled. That is quite a waste of a valuable resource, to be sure, and unnecessary. Cayce indicated that anyone could remember their dreams with only a little effort. He thought that a person who wasn't remembering them was simply being negligent.

Laboratory studies have provided substantial insights into what affects memory for dreams. Under ideal laboratory conditions, where a person can be awakened immediately following a dream period, about 80 percent of these awakenings yield some memory for a dream. If the person moves while waking up, dream recall will be less. The more time that elapses between the time of the dream and the time the person wakes up, the more difficult it is to remember the dream. Similarly, the more mental activity there is between the time of awakening and the time the person attempts to recall the dream, the less can be recalled.

Unless you learn to wake up after each dream during the night, therefore, the most likely dream you will recall is the last you had, which may occur shortly before you awaken in the morning. As soon as you begin to wake up, try to think about what you were dreaming. Don't move. Lie still with your eyes closed. Examine how you feel. Notice what thoughts are running through your mind. How you feel and what you find yourself thinking about are important clues to what you were dreaming.

Experimental studies have proved, and personal experience bears it out, that the motivation to remember your dreams is very important, perhaps almost as important, if not more so, than technique, as Cayce suggested. Having a specific reason to dream is helpful. Making an advance commitment with someone else to discuss your dream is also helpful. The motivation to remember your dreams expresses itself in your activities before going to bed. In one of my own studies, I found that when people write in their diaries the night before they are more likely to remember a dream the next morning. It seems that spending some time before sleep in an introspective activity not only is an expression of an interest in our internal affairs, but also prompts us to be ready to recall dreams. Placing a pad of paper and pen by the bedside is also expressive of a readiness to recall dreams. Finally, it is natural, when motivated to remember a dream, to imagine doing so when going to bed the night before. Mentally rehearsing the idea of waking up in the morning with a dream and writing it down is an effective autosuggestion. For many people, these hints are sufficient to bring about memory of their dreams.

If you are not so lucky, neither was I. I had to put in a

lot of effort and study to learn how to remember my dreams. I still do not regularly recall dreams without motivation or effort. I have learned that it is important to distinguish between the ability to remember dreams, which can be innate or learned, *but not necessarily used,* and the motivation to remember dreams, which may vary from day to day. Only if a person makes a persistent effort to recall dreams, and still fails, can it be concluded that there may be some problem—either a lack of developed skill or an emotional "block."

If you have trouble remembering dreams, here is my "effort test" to help you determine whether it is ability or motivation that may be lacking. Make a commitment to yourself that for seven days you will do the following: Have a pad and pencil by your bed. Upon awakening in the morning, remain still with your eyes closed for at least two minutes. During that time, simply wait to see if any dream memories come to you. Then, without getting out of bed, write down on your pad anything that comes to mind, whether you recall a dream or not. Write down any feelings or thoughts that went through your mind when you woke up. Write at least *one entire page* of material, even if you have to make it up. One of three things will happen: (1) you will remember a dream, and you'll be on your way; (2) you'll faithfully complete the seven-day experiment, but with no dream recall; (3) you won't be able to complete the experiment. If yours is the second result, and you find yourself feeling sad and disappointed, then it's skill that you need to develop. If you don't feel much of anything about the results, or if yours is the third result, then you're probably blocking and I would suggest taking up meditation. Meditation is known for dissolving emotional blocks. It not only improves dream recall, but increases ESP ability, as we shall see in the next chapter.

So there is good news. If you don't remember your dreams, then learning how to do so—either by developing the ability or in conjunction with practicing meditation to loosen any blocks—is going to increase your psychic awareness. Much of the same internal sensitivity that goes into learning to recall a dream is also involved in psychic awareness. Both require learning how to resonate to unseen targets until they "pop" into awareness. I attribute the birth of my own psychic awareness to learning how to lie still in the morning, being patient with my blank mind, until finally an image of a dream appears. Another component of remembering dreams is learning to be reminded of a dream later in the day by some "accidental" incident. Again, learning to be sensitive to the prompting of invisible factors (in this case, an unremembered dream that you are being unconsciously reminded of) pays off in developing sensitivity to the feelings, images, and other subtle promptings that are often the media of psychic impressions. So get on with it.

## A DREAM JOURNAL

Keeping a dream journal is the second step in working with dreams to develop psychic awareness. Get in the habit of writing your dreams down. Not only will this practice help convince your unconscious that you value your dreams, but it will also help you appreciate the psychic dimension of dreams.

Remember, the most common form of psychic experience in dreams is dreaming about the future. Learn a lesson from John Dunne. He kept a dream diary for several years, along with a personal diary of events and feelings during the day. Later he went back over the two diaries and compared them. He found many examples where a dream would contain an image that would later appear in real life. He concluded that it was equally likely for an image in a dream to be based upon an experience in the future as based on an experience in the past! This discovery led him to write his influential book *An Experiment in Time*.

I have kept diaries of my dreams and daily experiences for several years, and I found the same pattern as Dunne. *Without knowing it at the time of the dream*, I later discovered that many of my dreams were precognitive. These precognitive dreams weren't always about the future. Some were, of course, as Cayce has claimed—remember, he said that anything of importance that will ever happen to you will be previewed in a dream. Most of my precognitive dreams were about the present, but they borrowed from future experiences, often trivial, in order to construct their story. If I had not kept a diary and a dream journal, I would not have noticed these correspondences. Your dreambody, if necessary, can reach out into the future, just as easily as it can reach into the past, to locate the experiences it wants to study. Do write your dreams down, so you won't miss out on this fascinating example of the infinite reach of the mind.

## INTERPRETING DREAMS THROUGH ATTUNEMENT

What first attracted me to studying Cayce was his conviction that people could learn to interpret their own dreams. At the time he said it, that was a rare idea. Throughout history, dream interpretation has been relegated to experts. Long before interest in dreams became part of the "human potential movement," Cayce urged people to learn to interpret their own dreams. He argued that the symbols in the dreams come from within us, and thus we are the best interpreters of our own dreams. He also urged us to consider dream interpretation as a process, something that we were to engage in over a period of time with the dreams that we had. That is, instead of thinking that your interpretive efforts are only successful if you are able to come up with "the" interpretation, realize that simply the act of struggling with the dream is of value in itself. Finally, he stressed the importance of trying to find something from your interpretive efforts that you might apply, or try out in practice, as an experiment to test your understanding of the dream. He promised that our dreams are responsive to our efforts to understand them.

Our dreaming self is like a person in its own right, watching us, trying to determine our attitude toward our dreaming self. When that dreaming self sees us trying, it tries to help us by presenting dreams again, with a new twist, making certain symbols easier to understand, correcting erroneous interpretations, steering us in a different direction in terms of our applications. Jung came close to this orientation when he said that dreams were self-corrective to our attempts to interpret them; but he did not go so far as to suggest that they would become actively involved in helping us learn to interpret them. Cayce promised that help was waiting for us if we would but try.

Are there specific techniques to use to realize the messages of your dreams? Cayce taught two major tools: attunement and recognizing patterns.

To attune to a dream, meditate on it by sitting quietly and making the dream the mantra, or focus of meditation. I have found many times, with myself and others, that the following technique pays off: Begin a process of meditation, then have a friend read the dream aloud. As you hear the dream in the meditative state, all sorts of novel ideas about the meaning of the dream appear spontaneously. While still in meditation, speak aloud any ideas that come to you.

Another level of attunement is to relive the dream in your imagination, over and over again, letting the feelings in the dream seep in. To Cayce, a dream was an experience the soul has while the body sleeps. The soul guides the conscious mind through the resonating effects of the dream experience. The dream itself, then, is the best version of the dream, for, as the saying goes, "The dream accomplishes itself." That is, even though the dream may manifest as a series of symbols and strange experiences, that is only how we are recalling the soul's experience. If we attune ourselves to the dream story as we remember it, the soul's experience will begin to penetrate into our consciousness. As in telepathy or clairvoyance, where information is transferred when we attune to the vibrations of the object of knowledge, so the meaning of a dream is transferred to us while we attune ourselves to the dream.

Another level of attuning to a dream is to become

one with it, with each and every symbol. In today's popular parlance, this means you mentally become the symbol and role play it. Imagine being the tree, the dog, the running. How does it feel? What other images and thoughts arise? You may find yourself engaged in imaginative play with elements of the dream, having dialogues, changing the endings, and becoming influenced and creatively active within the story of the dream itself. Much of modern, expressive dream interpretation methods can be derived from Cayce's suggestion to meditate upon a dream.

## LOOKING FOR PATTERNS

Aristotle once said that in order to become a good interpreter of dreams, one needs to learn how to recognize "resemblances." Seeing resemblances means being able to recognize similarity of patterns. Cayce's major statement about interpreting dreams was to "correlate those truths" of the dream with those found in one's life. That is, find resemblances between patterns in the dream with patterns found in one's life. There are many specific ways to correlate patterns.

Take the dream as a whole and look for the pattern of the dream story. Search for the "theme" of the dream. For example, if the nursery rhyme "Mary had a little lamb . . ." were a dream, the pattern of that story might be, "someone has something that follows it loyally." The next step is to find a similar pattern in one's own life. Where in one's life has one noticed that there is something that is always there, following along? One's shadow? What else?

Examine the patterns inherent in the specific symbols. For a start, you might try to locate the source of the symbols. For example, is the image a memory from childhood? Something from yesterday's experience? Does it resemble something you were thinking about, a worry or a concern? Does the image remind you of a bodily process—digestion, elimination, nerve transmission? Plumbing and electrical wiring in a house can often be likened to the workings of the body. Does the image remind you of something from your religious upbringing? Religion is a more frequent source of dream symbolism than is generally suspected, even among people who don't consider themselves "religious." Finally, the source of the symbol may lie within the universal consciousness, it may be what is called a universal symbol. In the nursery rhyme "Mary had a little lamb . . ." the lamb could refer to Jesus. He is always there, waiting to be called upon, often neglected or sacrificed in favor of some goal of expediency, in the same way we often ignore our real, inner self in favor of looking good or measuring up.

The idea that you might have to study and learn about universal symbols should not discourage you. Although it does help to read widely in the world's symbolic literature, it is really not necessary. In fact, to do so often defeats the purpose, especially if this kind of book learning tempts you to interpret symbols by rote. If universal symbols can spontaneously appear in your dreams, independent of your ever having encountered them in your life, then it must also be true that you can spontaneously understand the meaning of the symbol without doing special reading. Often when a person has a dream with a universal symbol and becomes one with it, role playing that symbol for a while, some piece of the universal understanding that is contained in the symbol will filter into the person's consciousness. The universal nature of the symbol will pattern the person's imagination as the role playing proceeds. Dreams are a complete resource. According to Cayce, all you need do is attune to them, try out your ideas in practice, and the meaning of the symbols will be given.

## TEST YOUR INTERPRETATION IN APPLICATION

Cayce proposed that if you would develop at least some kind of interpretation of your dream, then apply that insight as best you can, subsequent dreams would be easier to understand, and would help you to modify your insight toward a better understanding of the truth. I had a chance to test this hypothesis with a group of two hundred A.R.E. members who participated in a twenty-eight-day experiment on seeking guidance from dreams.

The participants each attempted to solve a personal problem by developing a solution from their dreams, following the format of my self-help program, *The Dream Quest Workbook*. The program helped them develop specific ideas from their dreams concerning steps toward a solution to their chosen problem. They kept daily logs on various aspects of their behavior during the project. These logs measured the amount of dream recall; how easy to understand these dreams were without interpretive work; how much time was spent in meditation; and how much effort was given to applying a dream insight toward the solution of their personal problem. At the end of the study, we used these daily logs to provide a statistical analysis of behavioral patterns. The analysis confirmed a finding from an earlier study: there was more dream recall on mornings following a day that included meditation than following days that did not include meditation. Meditation, as we mentioned earlier, does aid dream recall. With regard to the dreams themselves, however, and how easy they were to understand, meditation did not have much effect! Dreams following days that included activities intended to apply insights from previous dreams were found to be much clearer in their meaning than dreams following days that included no attempts at application.

Learning to understand dreams proceeds like science: test your ideas with experiments and you'll gain insights, often in unexpected places!

## DREAMING WITH A PURPOSE: DREAM INCUBATION

In the study just described, the participants were practicing a form of "dream incubation"—actively preparing themselves to have dreams that would speak to their needs. They found answers to questions and solutions to problems by engaging in a repeated cycle of dream incubation, dream interpretation, and application of the interpretation.

Dreams speak to our needs, and sometimes to our specific intentions as well. They do so whether we ask them to or not; but when we do ask, we can quicken the process of becoming better acquainted with dreams. It is a common occurrence for someone to read about a dream phenomenon only to have that same phenomenon occur in a later dream. The person wanted a personal experience and their dreams provided one! That is a process of unintentional or unconscious dream incubation. To incubate a dream is to plant a seed about a dream, allowing it to sprout into an actual dream experience.

Intentional dream incubation involves consciously asking for a particular kind of dream, or a dream about a particular topic. Cayce frequently advised that we "dream with a purpose!" Forget the popular notion that dreams are random gurglings, or involuntary mental spasms. You owe it to yourself to learn from experience that dreams are sources of guidance. Cayce invites us to go to sleep being aware that we could be guided while we slept, so we might therefore think about what we want guidance about. In other words, he suggested that we look to dreams as a responsive resource, and thus that we approach that resource with forethought and preparation. That is dream incubation.

There are many ways to practice dream incubation. The way you spend your day, what occupies your mind, and where your interests are most intensely activated will have a great influence on your dreams. Dreams also tend to complete "unfinished business" and incomplete tasks. It is possible to incubate a dream without any specific technique, but simply by thinking about your purpose for dreaming all day. Engage in activities that pertain to that purpose.

My wife, for example, dreamed of the house that we should buy before we found it. How did she incubate that dream? Like anyone else, we made up a list of qualities we wanted in a house. We examined the real estate ads. We drove around town looking at houses and talking about where we would like to live and the importance of a house for our family's needs. On the morning that we were to meet with a real estate agent, however, my wife awakened with a dream of a particular house. It portrayed many details of the house and showed that it was located on a waterfront. When the agent took us to look at houses, the first house she showed us didn't seem like much from the outside. On the inside, however, it was exactly like my wife's dream. Looking out a rear window, we discovered that the backyard was on the shore of a lake! We were amazed at the uncanny correspondence. In the dream, we were happy in this house. We decided to stretch ourselves financially and buy it. Ten years earlier, Jim Turrell had inspired me by locating his studio through a dream, and now my wife had channeled a similar blessing for our family. Here a precognitive dream was incubated simply by normal actions aimed at trying to reach an important goal.

Another way to incubate a dream is to spend time before going to bed writing in your dream journal to develop a specific focus for dreaming. In *Living Your Dreams,* Gayle Delaney suggests that you write about your question until you are able to develop a "one-liner" version that goes right to the heart of what you need to know. As you fall asleep, repeat this dream incubation phrase in your mind, over and over again. It may well prompt a dream about that question. It has been found in the dream laboratory that what a person is thinking about upon falling asleep often appears in dreams that night. Whether you specifically repeat a specially phrased question or find yourself preoccupied with your question because of your efforts during the day, you will tend to dream about what is truly on your mind.

Cayce reminds us that dreams can take us into whatever region of life we wish to explore, provided that during the day we are making equal efforts in that direction. To paraphrase the law of correspondence: "As awake, so asleep, it's what's on your mind that counts!" But whether you intend to or not, the statistical odds are that you will learn of your psychic abilities first in a dream.

# 6

# MEDITATION: ATTUNEMENT TO ONENESS

*Meditation is emptying self of all that hinders the creative forces from rising along the natural channels of the physical man to be disseminated through those centers and sources that create the activities of the physical, the mental, the spiritual man.*

EDGAR CAYCE reading no. 281–13

*Telepathy and clairvoyance are not the aim of Yoga practice. They are by-products of this practice. Cosmic Consciousness and universal penetration are the inherent nature of mind. Individual mind does not feel its cosmic form because of impurities. It is only when these impurities have been removed that mind begins to feel cosmic penetration. This purity is achieved only through meditation and contemplation practice according to the classical system of Yoga.*

PATANJALI

EVER SINCE PATANJALI COMPILED the *Yoga Sutras* in the second country B.C., it has been known that one of the side effects of regular meditation is the appearance of *siddhis*, or special paranormal powers. In the years since, meditation has probably become the most highly regarded practice for the development of psychic awareness. Patanjali's advice concerning paranormal powers—ignore them, because they are a distraction to the true goal of meditation—has also survived as the common wisdom. When people came to Cayce describing all kinds of phenomena that occurred during meditation—out-of-body experiences, hearing the music of the spheres, communication with the dead, and so on—his advice was usually to let it go, and return to your meditative focus.

If one's goal is conscious union with the infinite, meditation is the most succinct model we have for the development of conscious psychic awareness. Meditation has been likened to the art of dying. It is practice in letting go of the physical world, of letting go of identification with the body. It is a way to consciously invite, slowly and naturally, a near-death experience. A person transformed by a near-death experience often finds psychic awareness a natural expression of the sense of Oneness with life. It is necessary to let go of old conceptions of oneself and grow spiritually to deal gracefully with developing psychic awareness. Meditation organizes one's spiritual development in a harmonious sequence, thus easing the transition from identifying with a finite body to accepting an infinite awareness. In other words, if you want to become psychic gracefully, allow it to grow out of the practice of meditation. This is the almost universal advice given by spiritual teachers.

## MEDITATION AND ESP: THE SCIENTIFIC EVIDENCE

How do we know that ESP is enhanced by meditation? We have laboratory evidence. In a survey of sixteen experimental tests, Charles Honorton, now of the Princeton Psychophysical Laboratory, reported that nine of these experiments provided positive evidence for the enhancement of ESP by meditation. He calculated that the odds against such consistent results happening by chance are 1 trillion to sixteen! Pretty good odds in favor of meditation. Let's examine a couple of these studies.

The first such scientific experiment was performed by

Gertrude Schmeidler, of the City College of New York. She initially asked students to try to guess the identity of ESP cards. The ESP results were poor. That test was followed by a brief yoga meditation exercise. When she retested the class with the ESP cards, the students were more than twice as accurate as before and showed a significant ESP effect. Her simple experiment showed that even a brief period of meditation improves psychic awareness.

In contrast to that simple experiment, one of the most ambitious studies of the effect of meditation on ESP was conducted by Karlis Osis and Edwin Bokert, of the American Society for Psychical Research. Rather than employ novices who had never meditated, they employed people who were experienced meditators from a variety of disciplines—transcendental meditation (TM), Zen, and so on. In this study, meditators met once a week for two-hour sessions. These meetings lasted for six months, so the study was based on not just one but twenty-five repeated sessions. At each meeting there was a thirty-minute meditation period. Afterward, they completed a questionnaire concerning what happened during the meditation. Then the researchers conducted two ESP tests.

The first test was rather unusual. Imagine it from the point of view of the subject. You are blindfolded. In front of you is something resembling a chess board, with five rows and five columns, totaling twenty-five squares. The squares are engraved so you can feel them with your fingers. You are told there is one "correct" square to choose. You are asked to "feel your way" to the correct square and put your finger there to signal your choice. Meanwhile, a TV camera takes a close-up shot of your hand on the guessing board, which is relayed to the watchful eyes of a person in another room. In front of this person is a similar board, with a red checker on the "correct" square. Although you can't hear or see anything, this person is "coaching" you, trying to urge you to choose the correct square.

The second test was similar to one used in the Maimonides dream telepathy experiments. The difference was that the subject, instead of being asleep and dreaming, was asked to relax and focus on thoughts and images. Meanwhile, in another room, the sender chose a picture at random to transmit telepathically. The subject's impressions were recorded verbatim. Afterward, judges tried to match these impressions against a set of pictures, including the one that the sender had been trying to transmit.

Subjects demonstrated positive evidence of ESP in both these tests. Among the many qualities of the meditation experience that were measured (degree of relaxation, serenity, concentration, intruding thoughts), the most important to ESP functioning was the factor of "openness and transcendence" achieved in the meditation. If the subject indicated that during the meditation there was a feeling of becoming one with the external world, of merging with others, of a feeling of unity with the group, of changes in the way of experiencing things, or of feelings of love, joy, or security, then that subject was most likely to give evidence of ESP on the tests.

This result should ring a bell. In chapter two, we discussed LeShan's work, which indicated that feelings of Oneness were characteristic of the psychic's state of mind, and his experiments in training people to achieve that consciousness of Oneness with one another, which resulted in psychic interactions. Osis and Bokert's study demonstrates the same connection between the experience of Oneness and psychic awareness and that meditation is clearly a path to that experience.

## WHAT HAPPENS IN MEDITATION?

Let's look in on a scientist studying meditation. Deep within the laboratory is a quiet, dimly lit room, with a comfortable, well-padded, slightly reclining chair. Some electronic equipment is nearby to monitor the subject in the chair. The scientist instructs the subject for this experimental meditation.

"Try to sit in a relatively upright position, so that your posture is balanced. That way, your body will not have

to expend much energy to hold you up. Now close your
eyes and let yourself relax. Notice that every time your
body exhales, it relaxes. Allow your attention to rest its
focus on the in and out of the breath. Every time the
breath goes out, it is relaxing. Every time the breath
comes in, let it be with the thought 'one.' Let yourself
think the word 'one' each time the breath comes in.
Make no effort, but simply let your mind think 'one'
with every incoming breath, like an automatic thought.
Your mind will wander. That is natural. Whenever you
discover that your mind has wandered, gently return
your focus to your breathing, thinking the word 'one'
with every breath.

"Just continue doing this now. At the end of the meditation period, I will inform you that it is time to stop."

With these simple instructions, the scientist has "initiated" the subject into what has been called "clinically
standardized meditation," developed by Patricia Car-
rington, of Princeton University. It is a type of generic
meditation, based on common elements of the various
schools of meditation. It incorporates the focus on the
breath, as in Zen meditation, as well as the repetitive
mental focus (the word "one"), or mantra, as used in
Transcendental Meditation. The use of this standardized form of meditation makes it easier for scientists to
coordinate their research efforts. Now let's go into the
monitoring room and watch what the scientist observes
of the subject's meditation.

Wires leading from the monitors attached to the body
of the subject culminate in various dials and gauges in
the observation room. A computer keeps track of all the
readings. There are many signs that the subject is becoming relaxed. The heart rate is slowing down, and the
blood pressure is dropping a bit. The breathing has
slowed to a regular tempo. Analysis of the subject's
blood shows changes in body chemistry, indicating that
the rate of metabolism is dropping. The brain-wave report is beginning to show the presence of the alpha
rhythm, a smooth wave of about ten cycles a second. It
comes and goes, alternating with the more typical beta
wave, a tight, muddled, and irregular wave associated

with normal waking thought. Gradually, the alpha wave is becoming the predominant pattern. First on one side of the brain, and now on both. The alpha report from the two sides of the brain then begins to show signs of synchronization as both waves move up and down together, in slow and steady harmony.

We are witnessing the typical pattern of physiological changes during meditation. The picture is one of quieting down, slowing down, and simplification. It is as if we put sand in a glass of water, stirred it up, and allowed it gradually to settle and clarify. What else might be happening? Let's listen while the scientist asks the subject what it was like to meditate, what happened on the inside:

"It was very relaxing," replies the subject. "Was I really meditating for twenty minutes? I thought that only a few minutes had passed. It was strange at first. I was overly aware of my breathing, and my heart seemed like it was beating very loud. I could feel my pulse through my whole body.

"At first it was easy to focus on my breathing, but soon my mind began to get pretty active. I would catch it and go back to my breathing, but I had to do it over and over again. I don't think my mind ever stopped, but after a while it just seemed different. Like the thoughts were somewhere else, I guess, because it seemed that I just paid them no attention. It was so restful being with my breathing.

"It almost seemed as if the breathing itself said 'one,' because it was so automatic. It was like I was hearing the word 'one,' not actually thinking it myself. The word seemed to change, too, sometimes soft, then loud, close by, far away, very big, then very small, and sometimes it seemed like it was other words, like 'won,' or 'un.' Then all of a sudden, you signaled me, and I realized that I was doing meditation. I guess I forgot where I was."

The subject mentioned that after a while, the focus word, "one," began to change. Psychologists who have studied meditation have noted that meditation has a dramatic effect on attention and perception. The subject is removed from most outside stimulation, as in sensory deprivation. The inner focus is repetitive, predictable—let's face it, it's boring. The conscious mind is used to having different things to attend to, and when it has to focus on the same thing over and over again, it begins to invent changes in the way it experiences it. Notice also that the subject said that the thoughts never stopped, but after a while they were simply ignored. They no longer evoked a reaction. After a while, the mind no longer responds; it just sits there.

Remember the exercise in chapter two, where you focused on a word or image and didn't let it change? Remember how your mind wandered, how the image changed? Then you noticed a background awareness that was simply a witness. Perhaps from that experience you can appreciate something of what happens in consciousness during meditation. Our mind's natural tendency to have something entertaining to attend to becomes frustrated during meditation. The repetitiveness of the meditative procedure weans the mind from its "addiction" to sensation. It goes through "withdrawal," and then, gradually and subtly, becomes unresponsive. More accurately, awareness becomes separated from its attachment to what is in awareness. In meditation, as in sleep, the conscious mind is retired, or set aside, as it is deprived of its needed sensations. If the meditator doesn't fall asleep, then awareness becomes purified, naked and visible to itself as a presence all its own. This quality of presence can be everywhere and anywhere all at once. Here is the beginning of the meditative experience of Oneness that will awaken psychic awareness.

## THE IMAGINATION OF THE MEDITATOR

What else happens in meditation? To find out, we would have to ask the masters, for science has not ventured too much farther than what has just been described. Cayce maintains that what else happens depends upon the purpose one brings to meditation. Research would agree with Cayce that what happens in meditation is not totally determined by technique, but also by intention and expectation. Masters of various traditions bring purposes that are couched within the language of that tradition. That tradition shapes the imagination of the meditator. As explained in chapter three, the imagination is the patterning aspect of the mind. The image of meditation determines the vibrational pattern governing the meditation.

Some traditions emphasize the developing freedom in consciousness. As attention is freed from attachment to sensation, attention can turn in on itself. Consciousness is freed from the body and leaves the body behind in its exploration of higher levels of spiritual consciousness. By realizing freedom from the body of sensory experience, we transcend death, for life is no longer equated with attachment to a body. Patanjali's *Yoga Psychology* is a good example of this approach.

Other traditions emphasize the spiritualization of the body itself. As we achieve higher states of consciousness, these elevated vibrations have an effect upon the body. As a chunk of coal is transformed into a diamond by intense and prolonged pressure, a human body is transformed into a radiating crystal. As each cell in the body attains cosmic awareness, a new being is brought into existence. Richard Wilhelm's translation of *The Secret of the Golden Flower* is a good example of this approach, and is similar to what Cayce envisions happening in meditation.

The more profound levels of meditation are a function of the meditator's spiritual imagination—the religious or spiritual tradition he or she brings to the meditation. The role of imagination in meditation was an important theme for Cayce. Not imagination in the sense of "making things up," but as the creative, pattern-making dimension of the mind. How we imagine meditation affects the experience.

I once heard Cayce's thinking on this topic expressed this way: "If you think meditation is a matter of making the mind blank, then that's just what you'll get, a blank mind—nothing!" Meditation is a journey. If you have no particular destination in mind, then that is probably where you will go—if you're lucky.

## A CLAIRVOYANT VISION OF MEDITATION

It is important to realize that in meditation, it is not the mind of the meditator that controls the action. In meditation we open ourselves up to influence. If we didn't, it wouldn't be meditation. Meditation is a surrender to a higher power. What kind of higher power might we be surrendering to? Cayce would have us *choose* the source of influence we are seeking. There is also a psychokinetic effect in meditation—mind over matter. Cayce saw that during meditation, psychic forces stimulate the body's endocrine system and the associated psychic centers. The source and pattern of this stimulation is important.

We can readily imagine, especially after Whitley Streiber's book *Communion,* the possibility that extraterrestrial beings operate out of invisible planes of existence. Through telepathic contact, they enter our consciousness. They want to experience consciousness in human bodies. More significantly, through the powers of their mind, with psychokinetic ability, these beings operate on our bodies. They are trying, unbeknown to us, to make functional changes in our bodies so that they can inhabit them, fusing with us to make a new, synthesized being.

Cayce never suggested that aliens from UFOs would try to enter through the chakras opened during meditation. But he did describe instances in which entities of deceased persons tried to enter the meditator, taking advantage of the person's psychological openness and the vulnerability of the psychic centers. In *Meditation: A Step Beyond with Edgar Cayce,* M. E. Penny Baker described a case of a man who began to meditate without regard for the spiritual aspects. He used techniques to open the centers, and found himself subject to influence by disincarnates. Gradually, one entity was able to take complete possession of his mind and body. When these psychic centers are opened in an unbalanced manner, psychic disturbances can occur. We'll learn more about the problem of these disturbances, called Kundalini crisis, in a later chapter.

Used correctly, meditation can open the psychic centers in a useful manner, to achieve a positive transformation of the body. Eastern traditions structure meditation to ensure that it progresses smoothly and constructively. Cayce's son, Hugh Lynn Cayce, and psychologist Herbert B. Puryear, both experienced meditators and students of Cayce's teachings on meditation, found the Chinese text *The Secret of the Golden Flower* to be one of the best Eastern sources on the meditation phenomena Cayce described with his clairvoyant vision.

Surprisingly, there is also a Western tradition that is a potential guide to the constructive opening of the psychic centers: the biblical book of Revelation. Cayce interpreted it as a promise, or a prophecy, of what will happen to any meditator. The end result is a transfiguration of the body and of the person of the meditator. The person becomes "God realized," in that the body and mind of the meditator are changed so that God consciousness can inhabit the person. Cayce stressed, however, that the person's own will is important in determining what happens during meditation. In order for the God consciousness to take charge of meditation, rather than some other source, the meditator needs to be willing for that to be the case. The imagination of the meditator, in its creative patterning of the psychic energies, is crucial.

## IMAGERY IN MEDITATION

Imagery enters meditation either implicitly, because of the meditator's background tradition, assumptions, or expectations, or explicitly, because of specific imagery techniques used in the meditation. Meditation is a psychic process in which energy, the spiritual or soul forces, affect the functioning of the body. The mind's use of imagery shapes how that energy will affect the

body. The creative aspect of mind, patterning the vibrations, determines the results.

In meditation, as attention is focused away from the
senses and back onto the mind itself, the meditator is
"raising the level of vibrations." This means that the
meditator is attuned less to the sensory level of vibration and more to the mental level, which is a step closer
to the spiritual level of vibration. "Letting go" of the
physical gives the mental and spiritual levels relatively
more influence in what happens. The imaginative aspect
of the meditator's mind then has a powerful influence
on how the spiritual energy manifests in the physical.

In *Meditation and the Mind of Man*, Herbert Puryear
and Mark Thurston explain this process by way of an
analogy. Consider the phenomenon of a photographic
slide projected on a screen. First, the light bulb in the
projector provides the energy; this is analogous to the
spiritual force. The slide in the projector patterns
the energy; this is analogous to the imaginative mind.
The projected image on the screen is the result; this is
analogous to the manifestation at the physical level. Our
normal waking state can be compared to sitting in the
theater with all the lights on. The picture being projected on the screen appears only faintly. Since we can
see clearly inside the theater, our surroundings affect us
almost as much, if not more so, than what is showing on
the screen. But when the theater lights go out, the image projected on the screen captivates our attention.
And so, in meditation, when the senses have been
stilled, the spiritual forces will have a greater psychokinetic impact on the body, and the nature of this impact
will be governed by the image chosen by the meditator.

Imagery can affect the body, as we shall see later, and
such imagery meditations have powerful effects. Some
meditation techniques involve using certain images, in
conjunction with breathing exercises, to open specific
psychic centers. Opening a single psychic center can
lead to bizarre psychic phenomena. Psychic energy
floods that center, with corresponding effects upon the
associated gland. The gland becomes overactive, and
begins to affect the rest of the endocrine system, which

tries to adjust to the trauma. Meditation on a particular center doesn't necessarily lead to becoming psychic, but in having psychic phenomena come to you!

Eastern traditions have exercises, involving visualization, chanting, and breathing patterns, for opening individual centers. Such meditations can be useful, particularly in conjunction with a trained practitioner of such methods, for operating on areas of difficulty in a person's life. Cayce indicated that karmic memories are stored in the individual centers. Opening the centers on an individual basis would release the energy of these memories, so that their effect upon a person would become pronounced. That is why kundalini crises sometimes involve strange "flashback" experiences, intense emotions, and powerful physical effects. In the hands of expert guides, such experiences can become transformative events. Cayce, however, consistently shied away from methods of growth that required a person to consult with an expert, and suggested instead methods that allowed people to come into their spiritual inheritance from within themselves.

Eastern traditions also point to the hazards of the single-chakra approach and emphasize that for purposes of spiritual development, it is better to open the chakras as an entire system, under the influence of the higher centers. For a holistic approach to spiritual growth, which is the context universally recommended for the development of psychic awareness, Cayce recommends that care be taken in the choice of imagery that is employed during meditation. He, too, advocates a pattern of awakening the entire system that is based upon the natural integrating effects of the higher centers. As we shall see later, Cayce believed that the "Lord's Prayer" was a formula for such a higher order integration.

Cayce recommended the use of an *affirmation* during meditation, a phrase or prayer based upon the ideal that the person wanted to govern the meditation. An *ideal* refers to a valued pattern that is used as a standard. The meditator should choose an affirmation that expresses the pattern corresponding to the meditator's highest value. It could be something as simple as the word "love." It could be a saying, or a prayer; Cayce gave several of his own besides the Lord's Prayer. He suggested that to begin meditation, the person repeat the affirmation until it was well established in mind, and then simply hold the *feeling* of the affirmation in mind as the focus, allowing the vibration of the feeling to resonate in the body. In suggesting that the meditator feel the idea as a vibration in the body, Cayce was referring to that process whereby the vibratory influence of a pattern in the mind has physical consequences. It is a process of tuning oneself to the vibrations of the idea. The imagination of the meditator, in the sense of the creative dimension of the mind, gives meaning—pattern and purpose—to the influx of the psychic forces acting upon the body during meditation. The effect, Cayce claimed, went right down to what he called the "rotary forces" of the atoms of the body.

## LIVING MEDITATION

Energy circulates through the body during meditation. This energy effect, however, should not be restricted to within the meditator's body. It also needs to be allowed to circulate outwardly into the meditator's life. Sitting in silence is really only one half of the meditation process. The other half is living meditatively. Meditation is practice, in a simplified mental environment, for a way of living.

Two major components of this way of living are the consciousness of Oneness and detached concern, or "being *in* the world, but not *of* it." Both of these attributes are developed in meditation, and need to be expressed during the day to complete the meditation cycle.

The ESP study showed how feelings of Oneness arise during the practice of meditation. Other studies have shown that the practice of meditation increases people's empathy for others. Empathy is a way of "being one with" another person. It has also been shown to be a basis for cooperation and altruistic behavior. Thus the feelings of Oneness developed in the meditative state can carry over to waking life. If you are willing to develop this frame of mind toward life, meditation can help you.

When we become one with life, feeling intimate with all that we encounter, there can arise a fear of needing to protect everything just the way we want to protect our individual, separate selves. That can feel like a burden. Accepting responsibility for others, as if they are a part of ourselves, yet not feeling the need to rescue them, is the attitude of detached concern. It combines caring with letting go. When we sit in meditation, our cares are expressed in the thoughts we think, yet we let them go. Meditation builds the capacity for detached concern.

Many psychics report childhood instances of traumatic experiences. A part of themselves became locked off in a safe, protected inner world. That inner child became the basis of psychic awareness and, when conscious, feels no boundaries with other people. Yet, wanting to "make everything right," that child psychic is burdened with other people's feelings. The danger of having or developing psychic ability without the attitude of detached concern underlines the importance of meditation in making the transformation to psychic awareness a graceful development.

## ACCEPTING MEDITATION

Don't be intimidated by Cayce's description of an ideal pattern of meditation. Just begin to meditate. The description of meditation given to our imaginary subject is a perfectly adequate set of instructions to get you started. The word "one" can serve as the ideal, because it can give you the feeling of being one with the universe as it breathes through you. Such an approach will be quite in keeping with the most universal aspects of the spiritual imagination. Don't worry about doing it "right," just do it. Whatever you think about while meditating (including wondering if you are meditating the way you are supposed to) is fine; let it go, and resume resting your attention on your breath.

Deep within us, the knowledge of meditation exists. The major stumbling block to "remembering" how to meditate is to bring a need for perfection to the meditation practice. I have seen too many people sit in meditation with a wrinkled brow as they try, so conscientiously, to do it "right." It is understandable, for our culture has trained us to approach almost everything with an achievement motivation. Yet wanting to be a "good" meditator, or to *achieve* the experiences associated with "advanced" meditation, is a subtle form of resistance against the essential experience of meditation. Meditation is essentially an activity of "being," not one of "doing." That's hard for us to accept.

Approach the meditation experience as one of surrender or "letting go." Rest your attention on your breath and let your Higher Power, however you imagine that Unitive Being, meditate you. Remember, the most important things that happen in meditation are not the things that you do but that are done to you through the psychic activity of the higher power. Accept meditation as a gift of Creation. Behind all the descriptions that Cayce and others have given of the incredible events that await you in meditation, the bottom line is that it is a gift of creation. Accept the gift and more will be given, much more.

# 7

# HYPNOSIS: THE HYPERSPACE OF PSYCHIC AWARENESS

*Hypnosis is only the revelation of the subconscious.
. . . Hypnosis is also communication with the very
limits of imagination and the unknown world.*

GREGORY, age sixteen, under hypnosis

EVERYBODY CLOSE YOUR EYES, get into a meditative state, and *watch* me." These seemingly contradictory instructions were given to a group of us in a demonstration of telepathic hypnosis by Dr. Carlos Treviño, a parapsychologist and hypnosis researcher in Mexico City. He had asked our group if we had ever witnessed a person going out of their body. No one had, so he agreed to demonstrate. As we all sat in a circle, Dr. Treviño said that he would go out of his body. We could try to watch with our eyes open, if we liked, but he said that we would see more if we tried to watch telepathically, by closing our eyes and observing visual imagery.

After a few minutes, Dr. Treviño asked us to open our eyes and to report our experiences. Many of us had "seen" nothing. Two people, however, said that they had the impression that Dr. Treviño had gotten up out of his chair, and moved across the room to the other side of the group. At their report, he got up from his chair, moved out into the center of the group and asked, "Where did I go?"

The two observers directed Dr. Treviño over in my direction. "Over here?" he asked. "Anything else?"

One of the observers—my wife—indicated that she had the impression that Dr. Treviño had leaned over me. He knelt beside me, put his hand on my arm, and asked me, "Did you experience anything?" I assured him that I had not.

"Do you feel anything now?" he asked. I said I didn't but he repeated the question. I was somewhat puzzled. He looked down at my arm, and my gaze followed his. Again he asked, "Do you feel anything now?"

People in the group started laughing. I was still puzzled. What was I supposed to be feeling? He looked at my arm and asked me again, "Do you feel anything now?"

Suddenly, it dawned on me: he was pinching my arm, but I wasn't feeling anything. From the look of the pinched-up skin, it was clear that he was pinching me quite hard. He snapped his fingers and I let out a big "Ouch!" I could feel it now.

He explained to us that when he got out of his body, he "traveled" over to me, hypnotized me, and gave me the suggestion that I would not feel anything in my arm. The snap of the finger was the signal to remove the hypnotic suggestion. He described this phenomenon as an example of "telepathic" hypnosis, or the induction of hypnosis "at a distance."

However I was to understand his explanation, what I still recall is the realization that I had been hypnotized outside of my awareness! In subsequent experiences with traditional hypnosis, using a trance induction, I discovered that I am not exceptionally hypnotizable and am quite sensitive to pain. Dr. Treviño's success at creating analgesia in me is a testimonial to his induction skills, telepathic or otherwise.

## HYPNOSIS AND PSYCHIC PHENOMENA

Hypnotic induction through telepathy is a little-known phenomenon now. In the late 1800s, however, it was a subject of much discussion, especially in France, where it was called "lucid sleep." It was considered sleep because the normal personality vanished and later had no memory for what transpired. It was called lucid because the hypnotized person was capable of talking, walking about, and engaging in normal behaviors. Yet this lucid sleep had some other strange characteristics, which ultimately led to the "discovery" of the subconscious and superconscious mind. Most important was the discovery that subconscious minds seem to be in telepathic contact with one another.

Hypnotic suggestions do not need to be delivered verbally to the person in lucid sleep. One of the early French investigators, Puységur, demonstrated this by thinking of the lyrics of a song. The person in trance would simultaneously sing them. In his demonstrations, he could help one of the observers get *en rapport* with the hypnotized subject, and then this observer could get the subject to perform actions simply by visualizing the desired action. Later researchers discovered similar phenomena, dubbed "the community of sensation." Two people were placed *en rapport* by having one hypnotize the other. When a substance such as an orange peel was placed in the mouth of the hypnotizer, the hypnotized subject experienced the taste. When the hypnotizer was pinched, the hypnotized subject cried, "Ouch!"

Other French researchers discovered that the entire hypnotic procedure could be accomplished through telepathic rapport. A notable case was that of Madame Léonie, who was the subject of much investigation. Dr. Pierre Janet, the noted hypnosis researcher, would mentally "send" a suggestion to Léonie that she fall into trance and perform some act. Observers dispatched to her house peered into the windows and watched. She was seen to fall asleep while in the sitting room; in one case, she suddenly got dressed and emerged from the house and went over to Dr. Janet's house, but with no understanding of what she was doing there at that time of night.

Lucid sleep also evidenced clairvoyant ability. In early research, the hypnotized subject could be blindfolded and yet read words and perform other such "seeing" tasks. Soon this "eyeless vision" was found to function over great distances. Hypnotized subjects could find lost objects and describe events occurring at remote locations. Some of these subjects became employed to perform these tasks, including locating lost children. This ability was termed "traveling clairvoyance." There seemed to be no limits to this supersensory power. It became commonplace to assume that a good hypnotized subject could read an object belonging to a patient and perform a medical diagnosis, prescribe a treatment, and in some cases telepathically heal the person of the malady. There were doctors who used the assistance of clairvoyant subjects to aid in the diagnosis of their patients. In this Golden Age of hypnosis, Cayce's psychic abilities in trance would have seemed almost normal.

## SLEEPING PROPHETS

During the 1800s, the psychic phenomena associated with hypnotic trance were primarily experimental oddities studied by hypnotists. People who evidenced psychic abilities were the subjects of the hypnotists. At the turn of the century, however, with the advent of spiritualism, the psychic functioning of hypnotic subjects escaped from the control of hypnotists and "psychics" became free agents, providing services and influencing the development of spiritual thought. Edgar Cayce, the "sleeping prophet," was one of these.

As a child, Edgar Cayce had already shown signs of psychic ability. He did not do well in school, and preferred the company of his own inner experiences in the countryside. The most-told tale concerns how, as the result of a vision, he discovered that he could sleep on a book and awaken with a photographic memory of its contents. At age twenty-three, he developed a strange malady that caused him to lose his voice. After repeated treatments by several doctors, he was pronounced incurable.

One day, a traveling hypnotist asked if he could attempt a cure. Under hypnosis, Cayce's voice became normal; but once out of the trance, his hoarseness returned. Another hypnotist who worked on Cayce had the same results. He was about to give up when Cayce, while in trance, indicated that he wanted to conduct his own hypnotic session. A third hypnotist hypnotized Cayce and gave him the suggestion that he could see his own body clearly and would describe the problem in his throat. In response to that suggestion, Cayce uttered what would become his trademark opening line for a reading: "Yes, we have the body." Cayce went on to describe the problem and prescribe a remedy, which was to use suggestions in trance to bring extra blood to the throat area. The treatment proved to have only short-term effect; another trance session was required to provide relief for a few more days.

Because these trance sessions were necessary to keep his throat healthy, Cayce began to give "readings" for other people. When his hypnotist put him into a trance, he asked Cayce for advice about individual patients. Cayce replied knowledgeably, and thus became a trance diagnostician before he realized what he was doing. He was apprehensive when he learned what he had done, but was persuaded by the helpful results for other people.

Cayce's story illustrates a pattern common to psychic healers: (1) he had an illness; (2) he was guided into a method of self-cure; (3) he discovered that his method also worked to help others; and (4) in order to maintain his own health, he used his discovery for the benefit of others. Anthropologists have noted this same pattern in their study of traditional cultures and shamanism. The popular biography *Black Elk Speaks*, the story of a Native American shaman, is probably most responsible for sparking the current growing interest in shamanism. A very important chapter in the story of Black Elk concerns his youthful healing, which was guided by spirits while Black Elk was in an altered state of consciousness. As an adult, Black Elk again fell victim to his illness. The spirits informed him that he was sick because he did not act out his original vision and offer his own healing as a benefit to others. Only by practicing his self-discovered method of healing was Black Elk able to stay healthy.

As a rule, shamanism involves an initiatory illness and a self-cure ("Physician, heal thyself"), followed by the development of a healing practice. A shaman usually enters an altered state of consciousness, in which he can see the patient's illness within its spiritual context.

Years before Cayce, there was another sleeping prophet who also fit the shamanistic pattern. The book *X + Y = Z, or The Sleeping Preacher,* written in 1876 by Walter Franklin Prince, tells the story of the phenomenal life of Reverend Constantine Blackmon Sanders, who was born in Alabama in 1831. Sanders, orphaned at six, had little schooling and could hardly write at the time he entered the ministry. Sanders suffered from "nervous spasms," with headaches and convulsions. When they ended, he would have no recollection of what had transpired; yet, once the convulsions had settled down, he seemed alert in a new way, conscious even of things far away. In this state, he—or the entity that identified itself through him as "$X + Y = Z$"—was a great finder of lost money. He seemed to know when people had died, could describe faraway scenes, wrote in Latin and Greek, performed clairvoyant diagnoses, and made prescriptions. Sanders was embarrassed by his seizures and afraid, as Cayce was for some time, that the things he did would tarnish his Christian faith. In 1876, twenty-two years after this phenomenon started, the $X + Y = Z$ entity announced that it would be taking leave of the "casket" (the term it used to refer to Sanders), and the appearances stopped—much to the casket's relief.

Cayce had not known about Sanders, who preceded him by a half-century; but he was introduced to still another "sleeping prophet," Andrew Jackson Davis. Cayce's biographer, Thomas Sugrue, noted that Davis's story paralleled Cayce's so closely that it gave Cayce "the creeps."

Andrew Jackson Davis was born in 1826 in Poughkeepsie, New York. In his youthful autobiography, *The Magic Staff,* the so-called "Seer of Poughkeepsie" described his own development in a time that saw the development of Mormonism, Shakerism, and spiritualism. He was a feeble youth, in body and mind, but evidenced psychic abilities, hearing voices and seeing visions of the recently dead. His clairvoyant powers were evoked by a traveling hypnotist and then developed by a local practitioner. In contrast to Cayce, he was not shy about his abilities and eagerly demonstrated them to the public. In the hypnotic state, he could read and see things with his eyes bandaged. He performed medical diagnoses, earning a doctor's degree and license at the age of sixty. Yet at the age of nineteen he had already begun trance dictations of spiritual treatises, known collectively as "The Harmonial Philosophy." He looked at his work as an extension of the late Emmanuel Swedenborg, with whom he believed he was in divine contact. Davis made prophecies, too. Arthur Conan Doyle, in *The History of Spiritualism,* said the best known were his predictions of the internal combustion engine and its use in horseless carriages and flying machines, the typewriter, and that spiritualism would yield a new religion.

## REPEATING THE "CAYCE EXPERIMENT"

Eileen Garrett's clairvoyant gift was discovered when she was inadvertently taken into trance when attending her first seance. She then explicitly developed her ability through hypnotic training. Al Miner, a psychic in Florida who channels the source "Lama Sing," discovered his psychic ability as the result of a visit to a hypnotist. When he came out of his hypnotic trance, he had no memory of the experience, but the hypnotist and Al's friends in attendance were stunned. Al had had an out-of-body experience, and described the troubles of a woman he didn't know who was a friend of another man who was present. A phone call verified the clairvoyant information. Hypnosis continues to produce sleeping prophets.

These have been largely accidental discoveries, but recent research has suggested that hypnosis can, under the proper circumstances, intentionally produce clair-voyant psychics. In *The Journey Within,* Henry Bolduc, a hypnosis researcher and past-life therapist in Independence, Virginia, tells of his work in what he calls "repeating the Cayce experiment." A critical ingredient in these experiments was Cayce's own description of what he experienced in his trance:

> I see myself as a tiny dot out of my physical body, which lies inert before me. I find myself oppressed by darkness and there is a feeling of terrific loneliness. Suddenly, I am conscious of a white beam of light. As this tiny dot, I move upward following the light, knowing that I must follow it or be lost.
>
> As I move along this path of light I gradually become conscious of various levels upon which there is movement. Upon the first levels there are vague, horrible shapes, grotesque forms such as one sees in nightmares. Passing on, there begins to appear on either side mis-shapen forms of human beings with some part of the body magnified. Again there is change and I become conscious of gray-hooded forms moving downward. Gradually, these become lighter in color. Then the direction changes and these forms move upward and the color of the robes grows rapidly lighter. Next, there begins to appear on either side vague outlines of houses, walls, trees, etc., but everything is motionless. As I pass on, there is more light and movement in what appear to be normal cities and towns. With the growth of movement I become conscious of sounds, at first indistinct rumblings, then music, laughter, and singing of birds. There is more and more light, the colors become very beautiful, and there is the sound of wonderful music. The houses are left behind, ahead there is only a blending of sound and color. Quite suddenly I come upon a hall of records. It is a hall without walls, without ceiling, but I am conscious of seeing an old man who hands me a large book, a record of the individual for whom I seek information (note attached to Edgar Cayce reading no. 294–19).

On other occasions, Cayce "felt himself to be a bubble traveling through water to arrive at the place where he always got the information," according to records in the A.R.E. library. In another instance, "he went up and up through a very large column; passing by all the horrible things without coming in contact personally with them, and came out where there was the house of records. It, the column, wound around on a wheel like the Rotarians have. He felt very secure traveling that way."

Bolduc asked, "Can Cayce's description of what he experienced while undergoing his shift to a clairvoyant state of consciousness be used as a guide to induce that psychic state?" Bolduc's idea is an application of the principle of correspondence and thus is founded on the logic of psychic consciousness. Here's what he did:

He began with Daniel Clay Pugh, a lay minister and auto mechanic, whom Bolduc had previously trained in conducting hypnosis sessions as well as in self-hypnosis. Cayce's description of his trance became the script for the suggestions given to Daniel. After Daniel was hypnotized, Bolduc suggested, "You will see yourself as a tiny dot out of your physical body, which lies inert before you." That was an easy suggestion for Daniel to follow. At the next suggestion, "You find yourself oppressed by darkness and there is a feeling of terrific loneliness," Daniel's face drooped in sadness. Daniel proved responsive to each of the remaining suggestions. At the end of the sequence, he was given the name of someone and asked to say a few things about the person. His responses were encouraging. Each time they repeated the experiment, Daniel's body seemed more adjusted to the sequence. He expressed less physical torment during the passage by the grotesque figures, and the clairvoyant information was clearer and more accurate. As a result, Daniel began to channel what appeared to be a universal consciousness called "the Eternal Ones." Bolduc reports that Daniel has since begun channeling readings for others and has built a reputation for accurate and inspiring work.

Bolduc's book describes a second experiment with a woman named Eileen Rota who ultimately channeled a source called "Pretty Flower." The account of the process by which Pretty Flower worked with Eileen to gain a fuller entry into consciousness is fascinating. Early in the work, Eileen, while in trance, indicated to Bolduc that Cayce's imagery should be replaced with imagery derived from her own inner self: rising up a flame. When Bolduc shifted to this image, the work accelerated. That parallels Cayce's development—when he, rather than the hypnotist, was allowed to design the suggestions, progress was finally made.

A word of caution is in order, based on another of Bolduc's experiments. A woman wanted to learn how to become a channel. Bolduc asked her to work with the preliminaries first, to master self-hypnosis and to use it for general self-improvement before attempting to become a trance channel. She was impatient, however, and got her husband to serve as the conductor. She began using the Cayce imagery to contact a level of universal awareness. She showed signs of moderate success, but began to suffer from a skin irritation that eventually forced her to give up the experiments. Apparently, opening herself up to channeling touched off unresolved problems within her own being. The case is instructive, and can serve as a warning against jumping headfirst into such experiments.

Bolduc's work minimizes the common notion that "fate" or "divine selection" is required for the development of clairvoyant ability. By showing that it is possible to follow a sequence of hypnotic imagery and produce trance clairvoyance in some individuals, he has broadened the pattern of psychic awareness from that of awakening as "sleeping prophet" to one of intentional personal development.

## HYPNOSIS *EN RAPPORT* AND TELEPATHY

Laboratory research has confirmed that hypnosis improves ESP. Hypnotized subjects are more accurate than normally conscious subjects at guessing ESP cards, and are much better at identifying the contents of pictures in sealed envelopes. Two unusual experiments involving telepathy in hypnosis have special potential for the development of psychic ability.

One experiment showed how two hypnotized subjects can spontaneously become *en rapport* with one another and thereby demonstrate a telepathy effect. Allan Rechtschaffen, of the University of Chicago, asked one hypnotized subject to "dream" about a specific target. In another room, a second subject was hypnotized and asked simply to "dream," with no specific subject suggested. In one case, for example, the first subject was told to dream about the image of falling and not being able to stop. The subject dreamed he was in a tall apartment building. A girl was playing a flute on a floor below. There was a mood of tragedy. The subject fell off a window ledge, falling slowly. As he did so, the girl threw him an orange and he threw her a copy of *The Waste Land*. Then the building vanished. Meanwhile, the second subject dreamed of being in New York City and hearing music playing ("Rhapsody in Blue" and "I Can't Get No Satisfaction," by the Rolling Stones). Suddenly, the buildings vanished due to the Depression. He pumped up the buildings with a bicycle pump, then jumped on a tambourine that turned into a tangerine. He then found himself floating upside down in a hallway. The two dreams were clearly related.

Another study, conducted by Charles Tart, explicitly placed two subjects *en rapport*. The telepathic phenomena were even stronger than in Rechtschaffen's study. Tart termed his approach "mutual hypnosis," because he trained the pair to hypnotize one another. One subject began by hypnotizing the other. When a certain level of trance depth was achieved, the hypnotized subject gave suggestions to the first subject to go into hypnotic trance. Tart suggested that the first subject have a dream that would create an even deeper trance, and to report this dream aloud so that the other subject's trance could also be deepened by it. They exchanged impressions aloud for only a brief period, but then went silent for a long time. Although they no longer verbally communicated, they were nevertheless in mental contact. The telepathic rapport was confirmed afterward when they discussed their experiences. Their hypnotic "dreams" were quite similar. They also reported experiences of "merging," where their bodies and identities seemed to overlap. An intense feeling of intimacy was present during these experiences; it carried over after the experiments, as the two subjects became friends.

Tart noted some other effects of these experiments. Each subject was now able to achieve an increased depth of hypnotic trance. They each became more confident as hypnotists, presumably because the hypnotic state became more personally real. The reality of the hypnotic "dreams" surpassed that usually achieved in hypnosis, Tart noted, which had an interesting side effect—the two subjects did not like Tart's interference with their experiences! Tart found that his earlier work with the two subjects, establishing the power of his suggestion to come out of trance, was severely tested during the later sessions of mutual hypnosis. Although he had explored only a limited range of the possibilities in mutual hypnosis, the phenomena had already gone beyond the experimenter's control.

## LEARNING TO ENTER TRANCE

When Cayce was asked about the usefulness of hypnosis, his response depended upon who was asking. Judging from some of his remarks, it would seem that he was in accord with contemporary hypnotists who recognize that hypnosis is a powerful, yet neutral tool, which can be used for good or ill. Troubled or unstable personalities can be attracted to hypnosis and use it in an unfortunate manner; but it can also be used to good effect as a therapeutic device or to develop psychic awareness. The value of hypnosis also depends on the ideals and purposes of the people who use it.

Cayce did indicate that the self-hypnotic trance is a skill that can be learned with practice. In *Self-Hypnosis: Creating Your Own Destiny,* Henry Bolduc provides the details and integrates the perspective of the Edgar Cayce readings. Many books on hypnosis can be adapted for the purpose of self-hypnosis through the use of self-recorded audio cassettes. In this manner, you can become the subject of a hypnosis session of your own design.

Some people may nevertheless find it difficult to learn self-hypnosis on their own. Hypnosis has a certain mystique—it can seem sinister or frightening; there is some concern about losing control. Hypnosis can also seem inaccessible or elusive. It certainly has been difficult for experts to define this state of consciousness. Learning self-hypnosis by oneself can therefore be difficult, because of the questions it raises: "Will I be OK all alone? Am I *really* hypnotized now?" These sorts of questions are not conducive to self-hypnosis.

One option to this dilemma is to get an initial hypnotic session from a professional hypnotist. The hypnotist can provide a sense of safety for the novice. It can be reassuring to be told, "Yes, you were indeed hypnotized—that is what hypnosis feels like." A hypnotist can also provide posthypnotic suggestions that help a person become more susceptible to autosuggestions.

Another option is to practice Autogenic training, which was developed by a pair of German physicians, Schultz and Luthe, as an alternative to the use of hypnosis for medical purposes. The autogenic state is meant to be self-induced, whereas hypnosis originally wasn't. It is a form of self-administered, "synthetic" hypnosis, which uses the typical subjective symptoms of the hypnotic trance as the basis for a series of autosuggestions. Since it asks a person to learn specific, concrete steps rather than induce the "state of hypnosis," a person can learn to induce the autogenic state from written instructions, such as those in Schultz and Luthe's book *Autogenic Training*.

Autogenic training involves learning that your body will respond to mental formulas. To begin, lie relaxed on your back with your arms at your side. Focus on your right arm and allow yourself to experience it as "heavy." Ignore any contrary sensations and repeat to yourself, "My right arm is heavy." Don't do anything to try to "make" your arm heavy. Just let it lie there and allow it to become heavy as you imagine it so. It requires learning that you can allow something to happen without making it happen. It is like learning to relax, or to fall asleep. It's not so much a matter of doing something as it is letting something happen, guided by your mental image.

After about a minute, stop and note how heavy your arm feels. Then wiggle your fingers and let the feeling in your arm return to normal. Sit up for a moment and try it again. Do the exercise for only about a minute, then stop, assess the results, sit up momentarily, and do it again. Stopping after a minute and sitting up between sessions are important components of the training. They prevent you from becoming lulled senseless and from forcing the results. The breaks also keep you focused on learning the specific task at hand, which is to allow your arm to become heavy quickly in response to your imagination. Learning autogenic training requires patience, not effort. If your practice causes you fatigue, or you ache or feel grouchy, better stop.

When you are able to experience heaviness in your right arm within a minute, then extend your practice to include your left arm. Focus your mental formula on your right arm for no more than a minute, then move directly over to your left arm, repeating the phrase, "My left arm is heavy." After another minute, stop, and assess heaviness sensations in each arm. After heaviness is achieved in each arm within a minute for each, add a third formula, "My arms are heavy." Practice this three-part sequence until you can achieve heaviness in both arms within thirty seconds.

Continue the training formula, inducing heaviness in each leg and then warmth in each arm and leg. The next step is to experience passive breathing, "It breathes me." There are further formulas, but the ones mentioned are sufficient to achieve a trance state equivalent to that obtained in hypnosis.

In this self-induced trance, it is easy to experience spontaneous imagery and vivid daydreams. When you give free rein to your imagination while in this induced trance, you are primed for psychic awareness.

# IMAGERY IN TRANCE: PSYCHIC RADAR

Dreams are the natural gateway to psychic experiences, and meditation is the supreme method of spiritual development that encompasses psychic awareness, but hypnosis is certainly that state of mind that makes psychic awareness intimately evident. Although it is not the first technique to try, and not for everyone, it is likely that if you persist in your attempts to develop ESP you will one day experiment with hypnosis. If you start with a good foundation, with persistence and practice you will surely discover the psychic potential of that state of consciousness once called "lucid sleep." Since it takes you to the creative edge of your imagination, and then beyond into realms you didn't even know you could imagine, hypnosis deserves to be called the "hyperspace" of psychic awareness.

# Part III

# THE SOUL OF THE PSYCHIC

# 8

# THE HOLOGRAPHIC SOUL

*All my life I have had an awareness of other times
and places. I have been aware of other persons in
me. Oh, and trust me, so have you. . . . Read
back into your childhood, and this sense of
awareness I speak of will be remembered as an
experience of your childhood. You were then not
fixed, not crystallized. You were plastic, a soul in
flux, a consciousness and an identity in the process
of forming—ay, of forming and forgetting.*

JACK LONDON

JACK LONDON'S STORY, *THE STAR ROVER,*
about a man who breaks the barriers of his prison cell to
travel psychically to other times and places is fiction, but
his character expresses Edgar Cayce's true experience
quite well. We are, he says, "a soul in flux, an identity
. . . forming and forgetting." London's phrase, "forming and forgetting," captures the essence of Cayce's
viewpoint concerning the development of consciousness—not just the development of the consciousness of
the person in this lifetime, from infant to adult, but also
the development of the soul over many lifetimes. We
need to examine this dimension of ourselves because, as
Cayce puts it, "Psychic is of the soul."

## THE CREATION OF SOULS

Many scientists believe the universe began as a black
hole that exploded outward. We still live in an expanding universe that is the offshoot of that explosion.

Cayce's version of the "big bang" theory is that God "exploded" into souls. Each soul was created at the same time and each soul is a piece of God; or, as Cayce once put it, each soul "is an atom in the body of God." God expressed as souls for the purpose of companionship. Each soul contains a miniaturized consciousness both of its origins and of the entirety of the Creator. Each of us is one of the souls that was created in the beginning. Cayce also maintained that the Book of Genesis was a valid description of creation, containing overlays of fact and symbolic expression. His view of creation integrates the biblical, "creationist" view with the scientific, "evolutionist" view.

When souls were created, according to Cayce, they were given free will and all the other attributes of God, including creative imagination and the power of manifestation. That imagination was the same as that by which God manifested creation, and souls engaged in a similar pursuit, for their own diversion. Through patterns created in the imagination, souls projected their psychic god force into material forms, primarily for the purpose of play.

As souls became more involved with material creation, two things happened. First, they focused more energy toward the physical level of vibration, intermingled with the evolving material patterns on the earth, and took on physical forms. In the process, human bodies evolved, and gradually developed the five senses with which to interact with the physical level of being. Second, as they paid more attention to the physical level of vibration, their awareness of the spiritual level gradually dimmed. The souls became hypnotized by the sensory reality of their own bodies and forgot their origin. Thus souls became "trapped" in bodies, in a sensory existence on the planet. Ever since then, souls have been engaged in the process of "seeing it through," learning through interaction with the material world a way to rediscover and reclaim their heritage as souls of the spiritual realms, as companions and cocreators with God.

The theme of wandering away from God, falling into

the illusion of materiality, and searching for a way back is universal.

Some Native American traditions include a dim recollection of origins in powerful space beings, and a certain sense of feeling abandoned in earth bodies. Plato's allegory of the cave, from a philosophical standpoint, evokes a similar theme. It speaks of beings who once lived in a world of light, but who wandered so far into the darkness of a cave that they lost the way back out. Eventually, they forgot the light, and mistake the shadows cast in the cave by the light outside for reality.

A psychological parallel to Cayce's story lends it another sort of symbolic validity. Consider the case of the lonely child who creates imaginary companions in his own image. They are not only creations of his imagination, they also reflect his own personality. Each is a projected subpersonality of the child. Sometimes, the imaginary playmates begin to take on a life of their own. They become autonomous and willful, they have their own agendas and want their own way. One day Johnny announces that he is "Aileron." Aileron denies Johnny's existence and Mom is alarmed. Then another day Johnny has become "Jakoda." Again, Jakoda denies Johnny's existence. And so it might go. It's natural for children to develop imaginary playmates, and natural for them to take on a reality of their own. It is also a meaningful analogy to how God's imaginary playmates took on lives of their own. Carl Jung developed a similar conception of the relationship between the image of God and individual consciousness, which we will explore somewhat later.

Cayce's story has another psychological parallel. Yoga psychology has maintained for centuries that conscious awareness tends to get lost and detached from its source as it becomes absorbed in the object of awareness. Pure awareness is quick to evaporate, as if it ceases to exist, while we become hypnotized by what we are attending to. It takes an act of intentional recollection to remind ourselves of that awareness, but it fades out quickly once again as we get lost in the stream of thought and experience. One purpose of meditation is to make us less forgetful of that source of pure awareness, to make it as real to us as the objects of our awareness. The soul must, in a sense, detach itself from materiality long enough to remember its essence as spirit.

Among the tools the soul uses to find its way back is the experience of dimensionality. Time and space, according to Cayce, were created as dimensions in consciousness to provide a playground for the soul to work through its hypnotic therapy session with materiality. Cayce often refers to the "skein of time and space." This reference parallels current theories about the mutual interdependence of time and space within the mathematics of a skein of yarn. He also uses the phrase "projected upon the skein of time and space," a reference to a theater backdrop screen, known as a skein, upon which the illusion of distant space is created. Cayce views space as a means by which the soul, through its senses, is able to maintain an illusion of separateness from God, and provide itself with an arena in which to find its way back to God. It is our means of hiding from the fact that we are within God. Similarly, time is our means of giving ourselves a stage upon which to work our way through materiality back to a conscious relationship with the Creator. In this perspective, the value of psychic awareness, which transcends time and space, is to help awaken us to our true nature and reality. This is how the development—or more correctly, the reawakening—of psychic awareness plays a role in our destiny.

## WHAT IS SOUL?

Each soul bears the imprint of the Creator. As such, it has within it the impression of the whole. Think what that might mean. If each soul contains the whole within it, then all knowledge is already contained within each individual soul. We tend to think of psychic functioning as an extraordinary feat because it appears to transcend our categories of time and space and the reach of the senses. But if the soul is created in the image of the

Creator, then psychic ability is not really an extraordinary ability, but simply a manifestation of the nature of soul. In fact, that is just what Cayce maintains in saying, "Psychic is of the soul."

Although God expressed into seemingly separate souls, each soul, in its own unique way, is analogous to the Creator's image. This view of the soul parallels a universal theme within metaphysical and certain spiritual traditions. Each soul is like a jewel in the Jeweled Net of Indra, each containing reflections of the whole. The ancient traditions also speak of "man as model of the universe." Sometimes this idea is expressed as "the microcosm reflects the macrocosm." It is an example of the principle of correspondence discussed earlier. All parts of creation can be found within each human being, and the relationship of those parts is analogous to the relationship of the corresponding parts within creation. According to this approach, the soul is that aspect of a human being that exists in correspondence to the entire universe, to God.

The Christ soul, according to Cayce, was created as the pattern for all the others. The Christ soul never forgot its unitary relationship with the Creator, yet voluntarily went through the cycles of incarnation, voluntarily got "lost in materiality," so as to be able to consciously find its way back again to conscious relationship with the Creator. Cayce maintains that the Christ consciousness is that awareness—which exists within each and every soul, and as a pattern imprinted on the mind—awaiting to be awakened by free will, of the soul's Oneness with God. Thus although the Christ is an individual soul, the Christ consciousness is a soul pattern in each soul; because all souls, including the Christ, were created out of the same mold.

Carl Jung developed a similar concept of soul. His term for it was Self. He used the capital letter S to distinguish it from the little self, our ego personality. Cayce made the same distinction, using the word "individuality" to refer to the soul qualities. Jung's concept of Self reflected the same duality that Cayce's soul concept contained. On the one hand, Jung described the

Self as if there were only one, implying that you and I were each, at the core, that same self. Technically, Jung did not equate the Self with God. Instead, he maintained that the sense of the Self was our symbolic experience of God. He implied that the image of the Self was God's imprint upon the human psyche. On the other hand, Jung said that each person's encounter and experience with the Self is unique. It is the task of each person, Jung believed, to come to terms with the Self in the course of a lifetime. He called that process "individuation," for it implied that no two people could truly engage this process in the same manner, even though we all would find that there were universal issues to confront. Jung thus portrayed the Self as both universal and individual.

By the end of his lifetime, Jung came to a view similar to that of the Cayce material concerning the destiny of the Self and its relationship to God. In his provocative book *Answer to Job,* Jung summarizes a lifetime of thought and research by proposing that the purpose of human consciousness is to help God evolve. Like Cayce, he maintains that God incarnated as a human in the person of the Christ. He also gave Christ symbolic status, meaning that the Christ represents a pattern for reconciling, or integrating, the polarity in the nature of the Self. He felt that the mandala, a class of symbolism that involves a circle enclosing a square, is the prime image of the wholeness of the Self as Christ consciousness. He found examples of mandala imagery in all religions. He interpreted the ancient geometric secret concerning how to construct a square of area equal to a given circle as expressing the challenge to bring into manifestation on earth the perfection of heaven, the mystery expressed by the mandala. Jung saw the destiny of humanity as the conscious realization of this archetype of wholeness so that God and human beings could exist in mutual, incarnated consciousness.

Given the radical nature of these views, it is significant that Jung, who has become one of the most influential thinkers of modern times, should have arrived at a theory—on the basis of scholarship, research in psychotherapy, and personal experience—that closely paralleled the viewpoint expressed by Cayce in his psychic trance. Modern thinking is following in their footsteps.

# HOLOGRAPHY: LASER PHOTOGRAPHY CREATES A NEW IMAGE

Just as developments in quantum physics have provided thinking tools for conceptualizing aspects of psychic awareness, so the laser hologram has generated a lot of excitement because of the thinking tools it has provided. The hologram gives us a modern way to imagine how it can be that, as philosophers and psychologists of the ages attest, if you look deeply into one person you can find the story of all humanity. But that is not all. The hologram is also becoming a model for neuroscientists to develop a new theory of consciousness.

A laser beam is created by use of a ruby crystal—a development, by the way, predicted by Cayce. The beam is an intensely focused ray of light. The waves of the light can be made to be of exactly the same frequency, and all particles of the light beam are made to wave in unison—all the light waves go up and down at the same time. The terms *coherent* is used to describe the quality of the light beam. The coherence of the laser beam is a critical aspect of the laser's ability to create holograms.

When a laser beam is cast upon an object, the light bounces off the object in all directions. Laser photography, or holography, uses no lens to focus the light reflected from the object that lands on the photographic plate. Instead, the source of light itself, the laser beam, is already focused. The reflected light is allowed to scatter itself on the holographic plate. The resulting holographic plate looks like a meaningless collection of swirls. However, when a laser beam of the same frequency as that used in the original exposure is now cast upon the holographic plate, a three-dimensional image of the original object is projected into space. You can examine this image from all sides, for a true, three-dimensional view.

To gain some appreciation of how the hologram creates such magic, consider the sound recording. You can record the complex vibrational patterns of a symphony orchestra by reducing them into patterns of gouges on a plastic record. When you run a needle across these gouges, the full complex sound of the symphony orchestra is reproduced. If the orchestra is recorded from two locations simultaneously, and both sets of vibrational patterns are reproduced, a stereo depth effect is created. Yet as you walk about the room, this sensation remains only to a limited extent. You can't walk to a place that sounds like the rear of the orchestra, but just a bit from side to side. The same principle works for the vibratory patterns of light energy. Typical 3-D pictures are created by two cameras that photograph a scene from two perspectives. When these images are projected upon a screen, and special glasses are worn, you can get an illusion of depth. In a laser hologram, the light patterns are recorded from almost an infinite number of locations, not just two; the effect, when reproduced and projected, gives the illusion of a three-dimensional object in space. It looks as if it is really there. You can walk around it and see it from all sides. The holographic image seems real—it resembles the objects we experience in the world.

The seemingly magical has become a thinking tool for transpersonal psychology because it provides us with a concrete, material example of the paradoxically holistic attribute of the soul. That is, you can break up the holographic plate into several pieces and take any one piece, shine the laser beam on it, and the entire three-dimensional image is again projected into space to be examined. The only difference between the image seen when projected from a complete plate and when projected from a piece of the plate is that the former is sharper in detail. Thus each tiny piece of the hologram, although distinctive in the pattern of its record, nevertheless contains a functioning version of the original image. Until the hologram, there were no material counterparts of the ancient notion that each person, no matter how unique, is a mirror of the cosmos.

# BRAIN CONSCIOUSNESS AS HOLOGRAM

In explaining psychic awareness, Cayce made the odd statement that the brain is capable of "resonating to vibrations." Can you imagine the brain quivering in response to sounds? Cayce explained that consciousness is not "in" the brain, but that the brain is a receiver of consciousness, much as a radio is the receiver of radio waves. His theory of brain function seems at odds with what we theorize about how the brain works. We tend to think of the brain as a mass of wires conducting information to and fro. Yet theories about brain functioning are changing. Holography has provided neuroscientists with a new model. Stanford University's Carl Pribram now postulates that the brain constructs what we experience in consciousness the same way as a holograph projects an image out into space.

Rather than thinking of the brain as the creator of consciousness, Pribram believes that the brain resonates to vibrations that are in a dimension outside of time and space, similar to Cayce's fourth dimension of ideas and Sheldrake's morphogenic field. As the brain resonates to these vibrations, the patterns of neural firings throughout the brain are decoded, just as vibrational interference patterns can be decoded. The result of these decoding calculations is the structuring of consciousness into the images and experiences that constitute the contents of consciousness. The brain doesn't create consciousness, but interprets it.

Pribram was led to this theory after futile efforts to locate specific memories in the brain. He discovered that it was possible to destroy large parts of the brain without destroying memory, and concluded that all personal memories must be stored in all parts of the brain simultaneously. When he was introduced to the theory of holography he found the model he was looking for. He postulates that the brain is like a malleable holographic record, capable of being momentarily imprinted, through resonance, with any of the holographic patterns in the fourth-dimensional vibratory field. What the brain remembers itself, to distinguish personal from transpersonal memory, are the patterns it has resonated to in the past. Yet it is capable of resonating to any pattern existing in the fourth dimension, and thus is as capable of telepathic experience as it is of sensory experience. Our sensory experience of the world is the holographic image projected by the brain's current holographic pattern. In effect, Pribram is echoing the ancient affirmation that the concrete world is illusory, that true reality consists of invisible vibrations that exist everywhere, all at once. The hologram has provided a modern technological metaphor for imagining this ancient conception.

## SOUL AS MEMORY

A hologram, then, is a record, a set of memories. A soul is like an intangible, yet real, spiritual hologram. Not only is it a replica of the whole of which it is a part, it is a memory, capable of reconstructing the past. Cayce spoke of the soul as memory. He referred to the "Book of Remembrances," the "Akashic Records," and the "Hall of Records" as that domain where all memories are stored. He indicated that the soul contains a record of all of its experiences, that the soul is built from those experiences. And yet, at the same time, all memories are "as One." The universal awareness is the consciousness of all those soul memories.

The story of an individual, told from the deep memory of the soul, is the story of the universe. To envision soul as memory is to appreciate our common heritage, our common reality in the psyche. Such was the vision of Jung in his respect for the archetypal nature of the psyche. He did not treat these archetypes as inherited ideas, or memories, but rather as inherited patterns of consciousness, based upon thousands and thousands of years of human experience. This inheritance, as the patterning force of memory, is not limited to nor primarily located in the brain; rather, its source is that fourth-dimensional domain of the creative forces, the realm of

Idea. Jung, like Cayce, felt that the best description of that dimension was *pattern of thought*. The human psyche is patterned by a shared inheritance existing in the fourth-dimensional "ethers," or in the nonmaterial "frequency domain," to use the terminology of the hologram model. Jung sometimes spoke of an Old Man, thousands of years old, existing within the psyche, who remembers all and has seen it all.

I believe I have met this Old Man of the psyche. In Switzerland, I was introduced to some people who traveled about the world in a van full of drums. Beating drums is a natural form of communication. A group of us began drumming and soon found ourselves in spontaneous synchronization, a multitude of overlapping rhythms somehow beating in harmony. Time stood still and we became as one mind. It seemed as if we had been beating drums together for all of eternity. Perhaps archetypal memory was awakened, because the consciousness of that Old Man was evoked in the drumming. I can still recall the feeling that thousands of years were contained in the moment, thousands of minds were one. Psychic awareness of the nearness of all other minds and the memory of all time contained in the moment combine in the soul consciousness of the Old Man.

The recollection of soul involves both the development of psychic awareness and "far memory." In his psychic trance, Cayce saw the multitude of lives of an individual, the past lives of the soul in its prodigal journey. In his waking state, Cayce was initially an orthodox Protestant in his biblical interpretations; in his psychic trance state, however, he asserted that reincarnation was a reality. Cayce eventually integrated his perspective on reincarnation, karma, and grace into his religious doctrine. But such philosophical issues, and his suggestions on how to recall past lives, deserve special treatment, for they are beyond the scope of this book.

# MEMORY IN THE MORPHOGENETIC FIELD

There is another sense in which memory seems to exist outside the context of individual brains with psychic, or transpersonal implications. Sheldrake's theory of the fourth-dimensional morphogenetic field, used to explain how new ideas simultaneously occur in the minds of different individuals, is also related to Jung's notion of the archetype and Cayce's view of the Akashic Record. No experience is ever forgotten, according to Sheldrake, for every experience is stored within the morphogenetic field. If enough people have a similar experience, then the pattern of that experience becomes strong enough within the fourth-dimensional field to influence other people to have that experience.

Sheldrake's hypothesis of transpersonal memory has been subjected to experimental verification. In one study, Sheldrake sent assistants around the world to test people in their ability to perceive "hidden" objects in two different pictures. These perceptual puzzles were similar to those in the Sunday comics, where an object is camouflaged by the way it is drawn into the overall picture. After determining the percentage of people who could discover the hidden object in each picture, Sheldrake arranged for the BBC to broadcast one of those pictures to their millions of viewers, and to point out for all to see where the hidden object was located. A special close-up view of the hidden object was exaggerated so viewers would be sure to see it. Sheldake speculated that through the process of so many people seeing the hidden object in the picture, the morphogenetic field corresponding to detecting that object was strengthened, hypothetically making it easier for other people to detect that object later. Sheldrake then sent his assistants out again to test the same pictures on new individuals, people who had not seen the BBC broadcast. He found a 76 percent increase in people's ability to detect the hidden object that had been shown on TV, but only a 9 percent increase for the hidden object in the picture that was not shown on TV.

As startling as these results may be, critics theorized that other possibilities besides a transpersonal memory effect could account for the results. A wealthy American businessman sponsored an international contest for the best experimental verification of Sheldrake's theory of transpersonal memory. One of the winners was a Jungian psychologist from Madison, Wisconsin, who showed that the Morse code is easier to learn than an equivalently complex "novel" code. The only difference between the two codes was that the Morse code has been learned by others many times before. Thus the results would seem to support the notion of a transpersonal memory. As the experiment was repeated time and again, the effect wore off. The novel code began to enter the morphogenetic field, making it as easy to learn as the Morse code. Other studies along similar lines have also supported Sheldrake's hypothesis. That something as brief, in terms of human history, as a one time exposure on national television, or an experiment training people in the memorization of a code, can have effects on transpersonal memory lends credence to Cayce's view that nothing is ever forgotten. Every experience is stored in a "Book of Remembrances."

## PSYCHIC IS OF THE SOUL

Socrates' ancient advice, "Know thyself," was Cayce's second suggestion for developing psychic ability. (The first suggestion was learning cooperation.) This suggestion has multiple layers of meaning. To know thyself exacts a price, but it also offers a reward. The price is that we must bear the burden of responsibility for who we are. We can't blame others. The reward is found in self-acceptance and the freedom to be who we are.

It is no accident that the various techniques used for recalling past lives evoke reactions similar to those obtained in the recollection of childhood memories in psychotherapy. There is reluctance, there is fear, there is pain—these are the blocks. Working through these resistances, reliving past experiences, accepting our role in these events, incorporating them into our personal histories, being forgiving and accepting, feeling forgiveness and acceptance—these processes lead to a sense of relief and freedom. There is also an expansion of self-concept, as our conscious identity now includes all that we had forgotten, and our history falls into place as a suddenly coherent pattern of meaning. Creative energy is released that enables us to live life more fully.

There are a number of routes to the transformation of personality that has often been termed "coming home": recognizing and returning to the roots of one's true nature. A near-death experience can have that effect; depth psychotherapy can have that effect. So can the development of psychic awareness, when constructively applied.

A near-death experience that increases psychic ability also awakens the realization of the reality of soul. A person so affected becomes less worried about death and self-preservation, and values love relationships more. It is interesting too that people who have had near-death experiences often see the memories of their lives played out for them. Furthermore, examination of such people by psychoanalysis has revealed that they have somehow spontaneously acquired the ability to "free associate," requiring an inner spontaneity of thought that usually comes from years of therapy. These people no longer hide from themselves, exhibiting many of the qualities that are the fruits of long-term, depth psychotherapy.

Depth psychotherapists find that people undergoing such long-term treatment emerge with more than simply an alleviation of anxieties and other problems. They develop a sense of trust in themselves and in life. They discover that there is some higher intelligence at work deep within themselves, contained in the natural flow of life. As they make contact with the soul level of life, they begin to have important dreams, filled with universal themes. Synchronicities and psychic experiences confirm and lend a practical side to this new sense of being. It is another one of the paths to the recollection of soul.

Of these paths to soul, Cayce recommended developing psychic awareness in the context of spiritual growth. As we learned in chapter two, he advised going one step at a time. Step one, as you recall, is to cooperate. Step two, as we have just seen, is "Know thyself." He recommended that this learning occur within the loving community of family and friends, to provide both support and honest feedback. As step three Cayce advised meditation, to allow the mind and body to become more receptive to the soul's vibrations. He also valued prayer, to redirect attention back to God as well as to help others. Finally, he stressed the importance of finding ways to put one's energies and talents to use helping others, especially the talents that emerged in the form of psychic abilities.

Psychic ability, according to Cayce, was a function of the soul's experience during many lifetimes. In a reading concerning the development of his own psychic ability, he described how in one life he was a soldier mortally wounded in battle. As he lay dying, he had prayed to be released from his pain-wracked body, and experimented until he induced an out-of-body experience. This learning had carried over into the life of the clairvoyant Cayce. Another life as a physician had given him his psychic speciality, medical diagnosis.

Cayce maintained that psychic abilities are a function of knowledge and skills developed and constructively applied. What we use is ours to keep. He therefore encouraged us to take a practical approach. We should look for psychic ability to appear first in those areas of life where some creative talent is already being used in service to others, and to go from there. His formula, then, was one part self-development, at the spiritual, mental, and physical level; and one part service, at the level of prayer and at the practical level of everyday interactions with others. In this way, one step at a time, balanced development is assured. Psychic awareness is not some new, superhuman power, but the natural expression of the holographic soul.

# 9

# THE INFINITE MIND

*For mind is a portion of the soul force of each
body, and allowing this to become more and more
controlled by the subjugation of the physical
consciousness allows this greater influence to
become more active.*

EDGAR CAYCE reading no. 416–9

SIGMUND FREUD IS OFTEN credited with the discovery of the unconscious. In truth, he was but one of a long chain of people who brought to light this dark region of the mind. In Aristotle's time, for example, the unconscious mind was thought to dwell on the moon. It was said to be immortal and common to all. The conscious mind was seen simply as a function of the body, and was assumed to die with it. In 1892, Thomas Jay Hudson, an American, published *The Law of Psychic Phenomena,* which outlined his theories of the subconscious mind and its telepathic and clairvoyant abilities. Freud was a latecomer, and restricted in his vision of the unconscious to repressed childhood memories. Much of Cayce's description of the subconscious mind is in accord with Hudson's treatise, which Cayce encouraged us to read.

It is important to appreciate the unconscious, because our conscious awareness is but a small part of the entire range of intelligent awareness—the tip of the iceberg. Basing our impression of reality upon this visible tip, upon what is available to the conscious mind, we mistake the impression for the truth. Underneath the sea, a larger reality exists. For example, the various islands and land masses of the earth seem to be separate. Yet beneath the sea, the truth is revealed: the land is one continuous surface, valleys filled with sea, mountains rising into the air. So, too, to the infinite awareness of the unconscious: all of life is one unified being. Much that seems strange or impossible to the conscious, rational mind is only too clear to the unconscious mind. When we lay aside the conscious mind, we do not cease to exist; instead, the vast perception of the unconscious mind becomes more immediately available. If we learn more about the unconscious, we may learn how to tap into the psychic awareness of the infinite mind.

## THE TWO MINDS

The phrase "being of two minds" connotes a conflict. When Cayce was once asked to define mind, he defined it as that which opposes the will. It seems like a strange definition; yet it refers to a universal conception of the nature of what we call conscious awareness, or consciousness. In his *Essays in Zen Buddhism,* the renowned Zen spokesman D. T. Suzuki wrote, "In the beginning . . . the will wants to know itself, and consciousness is awakened, and with the awakening of consciousness the will is split in two. The one will, whole and complete in itself, is now at once actor and observer." You experienced this competition in the will firsthand in the awareness exercise you attempted in chapter two. When you tried to maintain a steady focus, your wandering mind countered your intention. Cayce and Suzuki agree that the creation of consciousness requires such a split, the observer and observed within our own being. This split echoes the pattern of creation we discussed in chapter three, when we discussed the yin-yang symbol as an example of the appearance of duality as the means of creation.

As consciousness is created, the unconscious necessarily comes into being. As Jung once expressed it in the imagery of a dream, when he carried a torch, he created a shadow. When he turned to look at it, the shadow was always behind him. It is hard to see the unconscious, for it is almost a contradiction in terms. It also suggests we are not in total control. Yet we must acknowledge it if we are to become whole and extend our awareness into the psychic plane. Then being "of two minds" can mean "two heads are better than one."

## OBSERVING THE UNCONSCIOUS

An easy and entertaining way to take a peek at the unconscious is to make yourself a "psychic pendulum." Get a nut for a $\frac{1}{2}$-inch to $\frac{5}{8}$-inch bolt and tie a 1-foot-long thread to it. Wrap the loose end of the thread around your middle finger, with the nut swinging free on about 6 inches of thread. Hold your palm down, with the nut suspended beneath it. If you like, rest your elbow on a table and suspend the nut about an inch above the table.

Notice that the main patterns in which the nut can swing in a stable fashion are back and forth (either from right to left, or toward you and away again) and around in a circle. Now see if the pendulum will swing in one of those patterns in response to a question you ask of it. Begin by asking, "Will you please swing in the direction you want to indicate 'Yes'?" Be patient, and soon you will find the pendulum beginning to take on one of the swinging patterns. You can then steady the nut with your other hand, and see what patterns it uses for other answers. Good alternatives include "Yes," "No," "Maybe," and "This source will not answer that question."

When the pendulum has obliged you by going through its motions with well-defined swinging patterns, you can proceed to ask it questions. Start first with questions for which you already know the answers—that way you'll know your pendulum is at least as smart as you are. You might then ask it questions concerning your feelings about various subjects. Check your gut reaction to see if the pendulum knows your feelings better than you do. From there, you can invent other questions to ask your newly discovered psychic consultant.

Using a pendulum to answer questions is an example of *automatism,* one of the ways we can observe the actions of the unconscious. Although the pendulum seems to be operating automatically, outside of conscious control, it is actually moving in response to your unconscious movements. These movements are dissociated from your awareness, and thus originate in the unconscious. *Dissociation* is a term used in conjunction with certain altered states of awareness, such as hypnosis, multiple personalities, and automatic writing, where the operation of one window of consciousness has become separated from normal, conscious awareness. The dissociation was produced in the case of the pendulum because you focused on the pendulum's movements rather than on your arm's movements. Once the pendulum began to move, your attention became even more focused on the nut, rather than on the source of the movement. Through dissociation, or diverting conscious attention, the unconscious can be made evident.

## LEVELS OF THE UNCONSCIOUS

Cayce identified two levels of the unconscious. The first level he termed the *subconscious,* and the second the *superconscious.* Although the boundary is blurred, this distinction is important. When Freud "discovered" the unconscious, he treated it as a repository of repressed memories. Everything in the unconscious, as far as Freud was concerned, was at one time a conscious experience, and then repressed. He conceived of the unconscious as a pocket—everything it contained was put there by the person.

Jung challenged that conception of the unconscious, claiming that the unconscious never ran out of material. After it had exhausted its personal memories, Jung observed, it spoke in a universal symbolic language—in dreams and visions—providing information from a source other than the person's own experience. Speaking symbolically, he would say that we each have a cellar where we store or hide our unwanted memories; however, if the cellar is cleared and the floor revealed, under the floorboards we will find a concealed stairway leading down to a spring that rushes forth from an infinite and ancient reservoir. Thus a person of little education might dream of ancient motifs from myths of long-dead cultures. Moreover, Jung saw that these symbols were timely and pertinent to the person's current life situation.

Jung termed the deeper, universal "spring" the "collective unconscious." In Jung's terminology, to get to the universal layer one goes "deeper." In Cayce's language, one goes to a "higher" level of vibration. This orientation is suited to the connotations of the superconscious, and is expressive of the psychic imagination. Let's explore this further.

In a dream, Cayce experienced himself as a tiny grain of sand. His consciousness then expanded like a spiral, a cone-shaped funnel reaching out and up into the heavens, to become as an infinite "trumpet of the universe." In his psychic state, he interpreted this dream as representing an image of the relationship between the conscious mind and the superconscious. A diagram (shown on page 157) was given to represent the levels of consciousness. Also shown is the diagram that came in a vision to Eileen Garrett, to represent her impression of the levels of consciousness. The resemblance between the two is clear.

## THE SUBCONSCIOUS MIND

The subconscious mind is an invisible servant. It performs all sorts of tasks that would otherwise burden the conscious mind. One function of the subconscious is to perform tasks that have become habitual, such as driving a car. The subconscious also performs the preparatory groundwork to deliver perceptions "organized for meaning and ready to go" to the conscious mind; it also

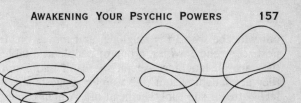

**Edgar Cayce's dream        Eileen Garrett's vision**

performs many memory tasks, such as calling people by their right name.

By the standards of the conscious mind, the subconscious is a genius. It is able to notice all sorts of subtle details that never appear in awareness; it has an almost perfect memory; and it is able to juggle all these things while performing calculations, organizations, and information search and retrieval.

The subconscious notices everything; the conscious mind seems blind and inattentive by comparison. Subliminal stimulation is a case in point. A message can be flashed on a screen so fast that we see nothing but the flash. The next morning, however, the material may appear in our dream. A recorded statement can be speeded up so fast that it sounds like a quick squeak, but again the statement will appear in the next morning's dream.

This supersensitivity is not limited to keen perception; it also seems to involve the abilities of a master detective who can discern subtle patterns. For example, British psychiatrist Morton Schatzman has shown that dreams can solve puzzles that baffle the conscious mind. In one experiment, subjects were asked what was unusual about this sentence: "Show this bold Prussian that praises slaughter, slaughter brings rout." One woman studied the sentence for some time with no luck. Then she went to bed. In her dream that night she hands a woman a slip of paper with the sentence written on it. The woman begins to laugh. The dreamer can't figure out why the woman is laughing, and moves on. In the next scene she is with a group of people at a table, and they are all laughing. Again, she can't figure out why they are laughing, but one woman suggests she would feel better if she took her head off. A man comes over to her and says, "Too many vowels, too many letters." When she woke up from the dream, she studied the sentence again, trying to see if the suggestion about vowels would lead to a solution, but it did not, so she went back to sleep. The next day, she wondered if "taking the head off" meant removing the first letter of each word. That resulted in a new sentence, "How his old Russian hat raises laughter, laughter rings out." The meaning of laughter in the dream now seems obvious.

In addition to its spectacular perception, the subconscious has an almost perfect memory. It forgets nothing—even remembering things you never consciously noticed in the first place (*cryptomnesia* is the term often used to describe this ability). Sometimes the feats performed suggest ESP or past-life recall. Thomas Jay Hudson reports such a case. An illiterate peasant girl, afflicted with a fever, began to pontificate in foreign tongues. Priests, brought in as witnesses, took dictation, verifying the languages spoken as Greek, Hebrew, and Latin. A physician, playing detective, traced her origins. It turned out that she was raised by a minister uncle who habitually read aloud. Among his possessions were books in the ancient tongues, and the exact passages spoken by the girl were located in them. Thus the source of the girl's amazing pronouncements was her subconscious, which had forgotten nothing.

## THE POWER OF SUGGESTION

In contrast to these prodigious abilities, the subconscious is also hopelessly naive and gullible. This trait is evident when it comes to the effects of suggestion. The subconscious takes suggestions literally, and without question. Cayce stresses this aspect of the subconscious, because he advises that we tend to become our own self-fulfilling prophesy. As he puts it, "As we think, so we become." The subconscious registers all our thoughts about ourselves, assumes them to be true, and acts accordingly.

We can take charge of this attribute of the subconscious. An extensive literature exists on what can be accomplished through the power of suggestion. Yet, the phrase is somewhat misleading, for the power lies not with suggestion, but with the capabilities of the subconscious. Suggestion is but the handle on the power, the means of communication with the subconscious.

We can also communicate with the subconscious through imagery, because it is much more visual than verbal. For example, try to make your mouth salivate by giving it the verbal command, "Salivate, salivate!" Now try imagining biting into a lemon and sucking out the juice. Notice the difference in effect? Communicating with the subconscious through suggestive imagery is often much more effective than communicating with it in words.

Properly addressed, the subconscious has a seemingly infinite range of skills. It has the power to control bodily reactions that would ordinarily seem out of reach. In fact, with the proper use of suggestive imagery, it is possible to induce the subconscious to control the actions of individual cells within the body. But the subconscious is also capable of other amazing feats of genuine creativity.

Hudson points out that the subconscious is capable of taking an assumption suggested to it and playing out all the implications. To illustrate, he describes the following demonstration of "channeling Socrates." A young man is hypnotized and given the suggestion that Socrates is standing before him. When the man nods in agreement, indicating that he "sees" Socrates, it is suggested that he may wish to ask Socrates some questions. He does so, and is then asked to repeat Socrates' answers. There follows an impromptu discourse, given with ease and clarity, which is a stunning performance of philosophical eloquence. Even knowing the speech to be that of the subconscious of the young man, the audience is inspired to take notes so as not to forget the illuminating insights. Such is one example of the "genius" of the subconscious, usually attributed to the power of suggestion.

## THE SUBCONSCIOUS IS PSYCHIC

The genius of the subconscious seems boundless. Perhaps that is because it is in contact with every other subconscious mind. This concept is worth pondering. Our language reflects it—"the feelings were in the air" connotes nonverbal, telepathic communication; "striking a chord" with another person recalls how we resonate together, each contributing our unique feeling vibration to the harmony we feel.

We often do not wish to have this contact made conscious, or at least publicly acknowledged. Perhaps it is enough that we recognize, at a subliminal level, that our subconscious minds are in sympathetic unison. As often as it occurs, it is relatively rare for people to talk about such feelings, except perhaps the rapture of romantic love. Intimacy between people often has a psychic component we choose to ignore. Doing otherwise would sometimes make us just too close for comfort. It is not always necessary, appropriate, or helpful to make psychic awareness an explicit focus.

On the other hand, did you ever have the feeling that someone far away was thinking about you? One of the most common experiences of telepathy is to have someone phone at a time when you are thinking of that person. The person's taking the initiative to make the phone call seems to initiate the telepathic process. When thoughts are directed our way, or even if a person thinks thoughts that are meaningful to us, we can be affected. In a series of fascinating experiments, E. Douglas Dean demonstrated that when a "sender" concentrated on the name of a person who had personal significance for a "receiver," an increase in the blood flow of the receiver could be detected. When the sender concentrated on the names of strangers, there was no effect. It is as if the receiver warmed up to thoughts about people he cared about.

It is through the interconnection of our subconscious minds that moods can spread. There seems to be no boundary, the possibilities are infinite. Maharishi Mahesh Yogi, the founder of Transcendental Meditation, proposed that if just 1 percent of the population would meditate, the consciousness of the entire planet would be raised.

Recently, his suggestion has been supported by research. One study located cities with populations of over twenty-five thousand, in which at least 1 percent of the population were registered TM practitioners, and compared these with equivalent cities having few TM users. Researchers found that those cities satisfying the 1 percent criterion experienced declining crime rates, while the other cities had a crime rate paralleling the national upward trend. This finding prompted several experiments. The results, reported in the book *The Maharishi Effect* by Elaine and Arthur Aron, were impressive. The experimenters chose target areas for temporary gatherings of many TM meditators. For example, the state of Rhode Island was chosen for a summer-long intensive course, attracting TM practitioners from the entire East Coast. International trouble spots were also chosen as targets—Nicaragua, Iran, and Zimbabwe—and large groups of meditators were sent to these regions to practice TM intensively. Various indices of conflict were compiled (deaths by accident, murder, suicide, divorce) for each region, covering several months both prior to, and after, the meditation gathering. Results indicated that during the period of the course, indices of conflict were significantly reduced from levels prior to the onset of the meditation. When the meditators ceased their experiment and left the region, the indices returned to their previous levels.

The poet John Donne said, "No man is an island." I wonder if he truly realized how we all swim together in the same emotional waters. We usually think of psychic awareness as relating to mind reading. Yet, the interconnectedness of our subconscious minds means that we

are closer to one another than our thoughts. It is almost
as if we inhale one another's feelings.

## WHEN THE SUBCONSCIOUS
## BECOMES CONSCIOUS

The stars are always in the sky, but we see them only at
night, when the sun's bright light no longer overpowers
their twinkle. So it is with the subconscious mind. It is
always active, even as we are awake. The pendulum experiment showed us the effects of the subconscious at
work. But actually to experience the world from the
point of view of the subconscious, to get behind its eyes
and look out through them, we must set the conscious
mind aside.

Cayce indicates that when the conscious mind is set
aside, as in dream sleep, meditation, hypnosis, and
death, the subconscious mind becomes the conscious
mind. It is like underwear that becomes outerwear once
the outer clothing is taken off. The conscious mind is
like a pair of eyeglasses that focuses awareness to such
an extent that the awareness of the subconscious, which
does not see in terms of separateness, distinctions, and
boundaries, cannot be apprehended. Take off those
glasses, however, and although the conscious mind goes
blind in the fuzziness, the awareness of the subconscious
mind is no longer camouflaged by distracting details.

The closest we usually come to appreciating reality
from the perspective of the subconscious is when we
remember dreams. The word "dreamy," to describe a
state of mind, seems to emphasize the malleable nature
of this awareness, with things changing into other
things, multiple perceptions superimposed on one another, and so on. Cayce indicates that our dreams are a
taste of what it will be like for us when we die. At death,
the subconscious mind becomes the conscious awareness, and we confront the shadow figures it contains.

When the conscious mind is extinguished, as in sleep,
anesthesia, or even death, it is still aware of the physical
surroundings. Cayce indicates that these are important

times to consider the relevance of suggestion. Recently, it has been confirmed that patients under anesthesia are "aware" of what people around them are saying. There have always been reports of this fact, as when a patient surprises a doctor by making a comment after the operation about some event that transpired during surgery. For a long time, the medical profession tended to shrug off these events as inconsequential coincidences; but in recent years, surgeons have taken them more seriously. In fact, Frank Guerra, M.D., of the Denver Presbyterian Hospital, has created the newsletter *Human Aspects of Anesthesia* to keep colleagues informed of recent developments in this area. Experiments have been reported there indicating that under anesthesia, a patient may be given suggestions to control the blood flow and to speed healing, with noticeable results.

Even after death, the subconscious continues to be aware of its surroundings. Thus it is apparently possible for a person to be dead and not know it. The Tibetans had procedures for encouraging the recently dead to "head for the light," and thus speed the departed on their way. New interest in the dying process, stimulated in part by reports of near-death experiences, has resulted in the adoption of similar methods in the West. Cayce advocated praying for the dead, and the Catholic church has had the practice of saying novenas for the dead. When a person dies, awareness does not instantly evaporate; the subconscious maintains contact for some time. If you are by the bedside of a person who has just passed away, you can continue to speak aloud, giving reassurance and peaceful guidance to the dead person to look for the "light."

## OUIJA BOARDS AND AUTOMATIC WRITING

The subconscious has a wide range of talents. Given a workable channel, it can apply those talents in some remarkable performances that are beguiling, intriguing, and revealing, as well as deceptive. Two such popular channels for tapping into this almost magical source are the Ouija board and automatic writing. The history of each contains some examples of inspirational psychic material as well as many examples of casualties.

In my own family history, for example, a Ouija board story stands as the most compelling example of the reality and mystery of psychic awareness. Years ago, my mother and one of her friends had been experimenting with the Ouija board. My dad, a postman at the time, asked them if they could get the Ouija board to do something useful. He had lost his wristwatch that day, presumably while delivering mail. When the women went to work with the board, it specified the intersection of two streets. That intersection, my dad noted, was not on his mail route but in another part of town. My mom said that since he had asked for help, he should follow up on the tip. They all went to the intersection and looked everywhere, but did not find the watch. Some kids were playing on the porch of a house at that corner and my dad asked them if they had seen a watch. "What kind of watch?" asked one boy. My dad described it and the boy led him to his house and returned my dad's watch. The boy had found it next to a mail drop box that my dad had used that day. It's common to think that a Ouija board picks up information from the subconscious. Since the boy seemed willing to give up the watch, perhaps his subconscious was the source of the Ouija board's message.

This feat is typical of the kind for which the Ouija board is famous. In Stoker Hunt's comprehensive *Ouija: The Most Dangerous Game,* he traces its use to before Pythagoras in the Western world, and before Confucius in the East. Both traditions used it to consult spirits. In modern times, it has continued to arouse interest and controversy.

In 1912, for example, when a woman named Pearl Curran experimented with a Ouija board, a person named "Patience Worth" appeared. Although Pearl had only an eighth-grade education, Patience dictated several novels and much fine poetry. Her novels, *The Sorry Tale* and *Hope Trueblood,* received rave reviews from the literary critics. Stoker noted than Patience could create excellent poetry on any topic, extemporaneously, upon demand. Once, however, when asked to improve upon the common bedtime prayer for children, which has certain morbid overtones ("Now I lay me down to sleep . . ."), Patience was silent. Two weeks later, interrupting an ongoing session, Patience declared (as if stating her ideal), "Let my throat sing a song that will fall as a dove's coo. Oh, make my throat dulcet, aye, and my words as the touch of sleep. Give me the tongue, aye, and the power of simplicity." After a long pause, this prayer emerged:

> I, Thy Child forever, play
> About Thy Knees at close of day;
> Within Thy arms I now shall creep
> And learn Thy wisdom while I sleep.

Perhaps the most famous Ouija personality today is Seth. Seth first came manifested through Jane Roberts's experimentation with a Ouija board. Later, Seth orally dictated a series of metaphysical books while Jane was in trance. One of them, first published under the title *The Coming of Seth* and subsequently named *How to Develop Your ESP Powers,* advocates the use of the Ouija board as a learning instrument to develop ESP.

Jane progressed from the Ouija board to channeling Seth orally. In that sense, a Ouija board can be an effective jumping-off place to begin developing psychic sensitivity. Yet in all of the sources Hunt reviewed, Seth is the only one to have continued to advocate the use of the Ouija as a doorway into the psychic. Others who have used it, even if effectively, have ended up discouraging others to do so. For example, poet James Merrill created his Pulitzer Prize-winning three-volume epic, *The Changing Light at Sandover,* by using a Ouija board. Merrill said that he saw too many friends getting caught up in it and swept away. Hunt reports one case of murder, countless mental derangements, spirit obsessions, and situations resembling spirit possession. Cayce also issued strong warnings against its use.

Automatic writing is just as controversial. Like Ouija,

it invites the subconscious to reveal itself for conscious scrutiny. For example, Anita M. Muhl, M.D., a psychiatrist who has worked with automatic writing as a therapeutic device, found that it is a powerful tool for her patients in discovering the subconscious mind. In *Automatic Writing: An Approach to the Unconscious,* she notes that it was not approached out of curiosity, but with the intention of healing. The material that emerged was examined, looked at carefully by both doctor and patient, and reflected upon. The purpose was to bring greater consciousness to the patient, not to diminish it in favor of greater subconscious activity. But when one simply opens oneself with abandon to whatever might come through, instead of following Dr. Muhl's ideal procedure, who knows what may happen?

The dispute over exactly "what" comes through the Ouija board and automatic writing has generally revolved around the dualistic polarity of subpersonalities versus disincarnate entities. What is unique about Edgar Cayce's perspective on the Ouija board is not his warning, but his dissolution of the standard polarity about the source of the messages. According to Cayce, the source is the subconscious. This means that it originates within the subconscious subpersonalities of the channel, the subconscious of other people, and from disincarnate entities. All subconscious minds are in contact with one another, forming a common pool. When the subconscious is allowed to speak, you can never be sure "whose" subconscious will speak up. In another vein, when Cayce refers to the *astral plane,* he is referring to that particular "frequency domain" of the fourth dimension where the subconscious dwells—both that of the channel and that of others—embodied and otherwise.

Carl Jung developed a similarly integrated view. He conducted a study of a young medium, from the time she first showed signs of dissociation until her mediumship ended, and published his findings in *On the Psychology and Pathology of So-Called Occult Phenomena.* To Jung, the question, "Is it a subpersonality or an entity?" would seem like asking, "Do ideas belong to the people who think them?" People are responsible for their ideas, for they express the person's being. Yet, ideas have a life of their own. Jung made frequent observations of the fluid boundary between the personal subconscious and transpersonal phenomena. He proposed that children often serve as unconscious channels of their parents' repressed feelings. In an approach similar to Cayce's, Jung viewed poltergeist activity as being a mixture of subconscious and transpersonal energies occurring in the context of a family relationship. He saw it as a type of mediumship in which, like a ventriloquist who didn't know what he was doing, the child "medium" displaces the phenomena onto physical happenings. The personal energy of sexual conflicts, for example, is "tossed out" into the room, where it runs the risk of being magnified by the presence of transpersonal energies (that is, "entities") of similar vibration.

A case in point is Matthew Manning, who became the focal point of a very clear case of poltergeist activity. He was led to try automatic writing, and when he wrote, the poltergeist activity stopped. The energy was diverted from the frightening physical events into the words that flowed from Manning's pen. He ultimately wrote a book about his experience, called *The Link*. Interestingly, the "entity" needed exactly the same thing that the subconscious of psychotherapy patients need—to have their story told, to be heard, respected, and released.

## MEDIUMSHIP AND CHANNELS

A *medium,* according to the old definition, is someone who communicates with the dead. Today, we would describe a medium as a *channel,* someone who communicates information from a source that exists in a dimension of being other than an embodied human. Cayce often referred to himself, during his psychic trances, as a channel. He also advocated that we all be channels to one another: channels of blessing. Both words, medium and channel, are technically neutral in that they denote something that serves as a conduit, a path of transmission. In evaluating channeling, the issue

Cayce would have us consider is not so much whether it is a deceased entity or an angel, but whether the information is based on a subconscious or a superconscious source.

People asked Cayce about their experiences in meditation, dreams, and daily life that suggested contact with deceased beings, usually relatives. Often these people wanted to know the purpose of the experience, if the contact was genuine, and if such contact could be used for guidance and growth. His response to these questions was fairly consistent: the contact was genuine and usually based on a mutual need or desire, often an extension of the relationship between the two when both were alive. As to their value, Cayce suggested that the contact had already served its major purpose: as an expression of love, or to reassure the living that the dead live on. He did not recommend further communication, however, but for reasons other than it was "wrong."

First, he maintained that the dead had no more insights to give than when they were living. In death the subconscious becomes the conscious mind, and can communicate directly with the subconscious of the living. To the living, such communications might seem like revelations. Second, he asserted that the dead need to let go of earthly concerns, make their way toward the light, and go into higher realms of vibration, as part of their passage into their own future. Often such entities have continued attachments to earthly experience, and this attachment is encouraged by a living person who desires to communicate and receive guidance from such an entity. He discouraged the mutual dependency that could develop from such relationships. He advocated instead that the living person pray for the dead and use other sources of guidance.

Cayce maintained this attitude in his own work, even though at times the spirits of the deceased spoke through him. In fact, at times some of the entities seemed to be angels or higher-order beings not associated with individual souls. On one occasion, for example, an inspiring voice identified itself as "Archangel Michael." It delivered a powerful message, and those in the room were stunned by the power and authority of the presence. Yet Cayce did not seek to further such contacts.

One of the more interesting cases on this topic was a mutual reading Edgar Cayce and Eileen Garrett did for one another. When Cayce was asked to comment on the spirit guides that spoke through her, he demurred: "Let them rather speak for themselves." As he explained it, the significant aspect of their nature was in the experience of Mrs. Garrett with them, that the spirit guides reflected her own soul development.

Ira Progoff, a psychologist who interviewed Mrs. Garrett's spirit guides at length, reached a similar conclusion. In his fascinating book *The Image of an Oracle,* he includes transcripts of his conversations with "Ouvani," "Abdul," "Tahoteh," and "Ramah," each a progressively higher order of guiding intelligence. He questioned each concerning the nature of their being. The conversation with Ramah, the highest of the group, was most enlightening concerning the status of these guides, and made quite an impact on Progoff personally. He concluded that these guides are reflections of Mrs. Garrett, and yet, at the same time, personifications of archetypal intelligence existing in another dimension, most especially in the case of Tahoteh and Ramah. His term for it was the "oracle dynatype," that part of human existence that seeks to express what is universal and transpersonal. Progoff concluded that each of us carries our own version of the oracle within, but that reaching to that level of consciousness was a matter of personal development.

When Mrs. Garrett gave a reading for Cayce, it was Ouvani who spoke. Ouvani confirmed the difference in channeling style between Cayce and Mrs. Garrett; that is, that entities spoke through her, while Cayce attuned to the highest within himself to view the situation under study. He also indicated that Cayce too had spirit guides that very much wanted to be able to speak. When asked to identify them by name, Ouvani gave an answer similar to Cayce's, that it was up to Cayce himself to make that determination. Ouvani went on to encourage Cayce to make use of these guides. He said that when Cayce was tired, they were already likely to speak on his behalf spontaneously. He also said that it would be a lot less demanding on Cayce physically if he would make use of these sources. Here Cayce received a suggestion that spoke to one of his actual concerns: the drain on his body caused by his psychic work.

Cayce asked his source about the suggestion, and the source indicated that it was for him to decide. Cayce discussed the matter with those close to him, and decided to continue as before, not seeking the guidance from the subconscious of any entity, but only the highest source within Cayce himself, his own superconscious mind. In a subsequent reading, Cayce's source indicated that this had been a good decision.

## THE SUBCONSCIOUS IS SUBJECTIVE

If the subconscious mind has a seemingly infinite reach, capable of responding from the interconnectedness of life and delivering to us personalities of amazing genius, isn't that what is meant by the *super*conscious? It does seem as if the subconscious is pretty super. But there is an important reason for making the distinction. Many people use the terms conscious, subconscious, and superconscious, or universal conscious, but ascribe all feats of telepathy and clairvoyance to the superconscious mind. That is understandable, as the subconscious has the reputation of being the "dirty pocket" of the mind, while its telepathic ability is overlooked or attributed to the superconscious. There is a problem, however, with this formulation. Not only does it neglect a major attribute of psychic awareness, but it misleads one into assuming that psychically perceived information must be accurate or unbiased. That assumption can have some negative consequences, because the subconscious is subjective.

Cayce described the subconscious as the mediator between consciousness and the superconscious. The subconscious gets information from both ends of the spectrum. Information obtained through the subconscious—even psychic information—will nevertheless be processed in terms of thought patterns stored within the subconscious. In other words, the subconscious is a biased perceiver, for its perceptions are colored and shaped by the accumulation of suggestions and memories planted in it.

Most spontaneous cases of ESP show evidence of selectivity based upon the needs and interests of the person involved. The death of a loved one, for example, is a frequent stimulus for an ESP experience. Here the relevance for the individual is obvious. Psychoanalysts who have studied the ESP experience of their patients have repeatedly found that *what* gets perceived psychically is a function of the patient's needs and interests. For example, it is common for patients to have dreams that contain, unknown to them, telepathic information about the therapist's private life. Jules Eisenbud, one of the most prominent of the psychoanalytic investigators of the paranormal, cites many examples in *Psi and Psychoanalysis*. On one occasion, several different patients presented to Dr. Eisenbud a dream that contained psychic information about him. Even more interesting was the fact that each patient had perceived something different. Each had tuned into an aspect of Dr. Eisenbud's life that was particularly meaningful and relevant to the patient's own struggles, issues, needs, and wishes. Furthermore, the factual information that appeared in the dreams was dressed with clothing from each patient's own mental patterns. Thus *what* was seen with ESP, and *how* it was portrayed, were functions of the perceiver. This influence of personal shaping in ESP is no different from what occurs in ordinary perception.

## THE SUPERCONSCIOUS

Jung called the area of the mind that contains the pure archetypes the *collective unconscious* or the *objective unconscious*, to distinguish it from the subjective, personal unconscious. Whereas the subconscious is subjective, the superconscious is objective—some call it *im*personal. Cayce placed the superconscious mind at the division between the Oneness, or God, and the individuality of the souls. It is like the soul's pure consciousness, as it was in the beginning, before it began to create distance between itself and the Creator. Remember the background awareness—the Silent Witness—we encountered in our experiment in chapter two? The superconscious is like the Silent Witness of the soul's primary consciousness, the subconscious mind. As the soul peers out through the window of the subconscious mind, in the background the superconscious mind is the soul's Silent Witness. Whereas the subconscious mind is affected by memories of past lives, the superconscious has the impersonal record of those experiences. It is the superconscious mind that can "read" the Akashic Records of all souls.

The superconscious mind is only active as an influence, according to Cayce, when we lay aside the conscious mind to make the subconscious mind the active consciousness. When the subconscious becomes the conscious mind, then the superconscious assumes the position of the subconscious mind. It is during those times that the superconscious can break through, in the same way that the subconscious can break through to the conscious mind when it is awake.

The imprint of the superconscious mind is commonplace in dreams. For example, the universal theme of death is often expressed as a return to the Great Mother, from where we originated. There is no one content to express that universal theme. Rather, when that universal theme is activated in a person's life, a particular image that fits the pattern will emerge from the person's subconscious.

For example, the universal return theme might be activated if you are undergoing a depression as part of a renewal cycle, in which the old must die in order for the new to be born. You may dream of falling into a hole, an image derived from such personal experiences as losing something down a hole, or a burial. The pattern is universal; the specific image that expresses the pattern is personal and subjective. Here the superconscious influence is indirect. "Big" dreams, however, involve universal symbols and less personal imagery. If your superconscious is speaking, you might dream of falling through a hole that goes all the way through the earth, and descending into a black underworld where your being is dissolved into a billion droplets of dark tears, absorbed into the womb of the Great Goddess. Such a dream reflects more objectively the pure symbology of the superconscious mind.

If we want to experience the superconscious level, according to Cayce, we must do more than set aside the conscious mind. First, it is important to be conscious of the ideals that you wish to have patterning your life, because the superconscious mind is the domain of ideals in their creative patterning function. The struggle to make an ideal a practical reality activates the energy of the superconscious mind. Second, it is important to find a way to live your life that simultaneously expresses your individuality and serves the needs of others while supporting their individuality. The superconscious mind is a level of being in which Oneness and individuality are integrated and synonymous, so to live this way is to live in attunement with the nature of the superconscious mind. Finally, you must properly honor your own subjectivity so that it ceases to call out for attention. This allows the universal level more opportunity for influence. Regular meditation and regular use of the hypnotic state for assimilating subjective imagery have been found to increase the frequency of universal imagery in dreams. When you take on some of the task of digesting subjective issues, you give some relief to the subconscious mind, allowing it more receptivity to the superconscious.

## THE INFINITE MIND

As William Blake reminded us, "If the doors of perception were cleansed, everything would appear as it really is: infinite." The boundaries of the mind are the bound-

aries of the imagination—there are none, except those
that you have set for yourself. We can project our imagination toward the infinite, as when Cayce suggests we
ponder our highest ideals, and find ourselves pulled
along behind. The imagination is like a grappling hook
to the outer reaches of the mind. It is also like a deep
wellspring, bubbling up with samples from the infinite
depths of the mind.

When you remove your Cartesian "head," the one
that separates mind and nature, you find a greater "I
am." Hold steady in the awareness of the Silent Witness. It embraces the full circle of the soul's mind, from
the endless patterns of the imagination within, to the
endless reflections of the Divine mind in all of creation.
The "here and now" mind of ordinary experience, as
William Blake reminds us, is potentially infinite, would
we but pause to notice. If we get quieter still, shift to the
subconscious, and allow ourselves to be sensitive to its
subtle promptings, new dimensions of infinite scope are
within reach. Explore meditation and hypnosis: they
scale the heights and plumb the depths of the mind. Or
abandon consciousness altogether and take a nap, for in
dreams we can experience still other dimensions of our
existence. And then, there is deep, dreamless sleep—the
state of consciousness most naturally in harmony with
the original, infinite mind.

# 10

# THE BODY OF PSYCHIC AWARENESS

*In this very body, six feet in length, with its sense-impressions and its thoughts and ideas, are the world, the origin of the world, and likewise the Way that leads to the ceasing thereof.*

BUDDHA

*Whenever there is the opening, then, of the lyden (Leydig) center and the kundaline forces from along the pineal, we find that there are visions of things to come, of things that are happening.*

EDGAR CAYCE reading no. 4087–1

WE ARE IN THE midst of a revolution. It is occurring in one of the most established, conservative enterprises in the Western world: the field of medicine. Striking at an intimate and vulnerable dimension of our lives, it will have profound impact upon how we view the world and how we live in it. The revolution, slow to gain adherents, was begun quietly by Edgar Cayce, the father of holistic health care based upon a knowledge of how the mind affects the body.

Cayce's leadership was recognized by the *Journal of the American Medical Association,* March 16, 1979, whose editor, John P. Callan, M.D., wrote, "The roots of present-day holism probably go back 100 years to the birth of Edgar Cayce in Hopkinsville, KY." Many of the exciting developments in contemporary medicine were presaged by Cayce in his psychic readings. Not just the general notion that the whole person needs to be considered when thinking about health, but very specific facts and concepts about the workings of the body, especially the influence of mental factors upon bodily conditions. It is in this area that Cayce's psychic readings are generally regarded as having achieved their most extensive validation, especially in the past twenty to thirty years. His views concerning the role of the body in psychic awareness are also valid.

As we have seen, Cayce's approach to developing psychic awareness focuses on learning to tune to vibrations, to set aside the conscious mind, and the value of high ideals; but he also emphasized the importance of the body. The body is the "temple" where we encounter the psychic energies. We can think of the body as the "instrument" of psychic awareness. Although the music itself is the message, that music must be expressed through vibrations. The musical instrument communicates the vibrations. If the instrument is not in good shape, it resonates to the vibrations in less than a perfect manner, and thus distorts the music. Psychic awareness is of the soul; but the soul finds itself projected into earth, where it expresses itself through the vehicle of a body. Thus we must examine the body of psychic awareness.

## THE BODY CORRESPONDS TO THE SOUL

The body is like a historical artifact that signals, to those who can see, a clue as to the nature of the originator. The body is the physical residue of the soul's expression as the vibrational energy of the soul has been patterned by images created in the mind. In Cayce's perspective on creation, as souls became hypnotized by materiality, they developed bodies and became "trapped" in them. Yet the body is not simply the symptom of this hypnotic entanglement; it is also the symbol of what has become entrapped. The body thus has a correspondence with the soul and points to it. According to the law of correspondence discussed in chapter three ("As above, so below"), the body is like a physical image of the soul, as that which was created in the image of the Creator.

Correspondence has many dimensions. For example, our posture reflects our mood. A sad person may stoop or slouch, a happy person may walk tall. You can read a person's feelings from how the body expresses itself through posture. Handwriting is another physical expression of the inner person, as graphologists will tell us. The structure of the physical reflects the patterns of the spiritual energy, as evidenced in palmistry and foot reflexology.

It is important to note that correspondences can work both ways. According to Cayce, not only do the spiritual and mental affect the appearance of the physical, but you can also affect the mental and spiritual levels by changing the physical. In other words, if you are feeling blue, and your head is hung over, then lift your head and your spirits will improve. The new "body therapies" are an expression of this orientation, and there is some evidence for this physical-psychological effect. Recently, a study was conducted to determine the effect of different walking styles upon mood. Researchers assessed subjects' moods by means of a questionnaire, and then instructed them to go for a walk. Some people were instructed to walk slowly and to shuffle their feet; others were told to walk briskly, with their heads up. After the walk, their moods were again assessed. The people who had walked with the slow, shuffling gait became depressed, while the people who had walked briskly were more cheerful. This is but a simple demonstration of a principle that is applied widely in the Cayce readings. He suggested purifying the body to become purer in spirit. Thus we can gain access to the soul, and its psychic ability, through our relationship with the body.

## THE THREE BODIES

Cayce was a master of perceiving correspondences and recognizing patterns. When it came to the levels of being of the soul, he pointed to a number of correspondences. In this three-dimensional, physical world, the soul manifests in patterns of three. He stressed the fundamental principle of the law of Oneness—that all attributes of the soul are actually all aspects of the same unitary reality—but he realized that "earthlings" naturally relate to the Oneness in terms of trinities, or patterns of three. The first pattern of three is that soul is spirit, mind, and body. Spirit is energy, mind is pattern, and body is physical form. The second threesome concerns the mind: superconscious, subconscious, and conscious.

The soul expresses itself through all three bodies, and each corresponds to a different level of mind. The superconscious mind expresses itself in the form of a *soul body,* which is also called the *spirit body,* the *energy body,* and the *causal body.* The subconscious mind expresses itself in the form of an *astral body,* also called the *mental body* or the *emotional body.* The conscious mind expresses itself in the form of the *physical body.* The two nonphysical bodies are generically termed *etheric* bodies, which connotes a gaseouslike, near invisible level of reality. Remember that in Cayce's view, our physical body is like a precipitate that condenses out of higher levels of vibration, much as raindrops condense out of water vapor. The etheric bodies are the noncondensed forms of the body.

*Soul Body.* The purest, or highest, or most basic form of being, according to Cayce, is energy, then pattern, and finally form. Thus the basic body—the soul body—is called the energy body or the spirit body. Its other name, the causal body, reflects the recognition that the energy level is the prime cause of the other bodies. The soul body is the most "real" of the bodies, because what is real does not die. We can burn a book, but we can't destroy the ideas in it, for the ideas are more real than the book. In the same way, a physical body can be destroyed, but the etheric bodies, the soul and astral bodies, are not destroyed.

This effect is seen in Kirlian photography, a technique that attempts to photograph the energy field of organic matter. This may be, for plants, the equivalent of the etheric body for people. The etheric body can only be seen psychically. It is what Cayce and other psychic and spiritual metaphysicians call the *aura*.

*Mental Body.* The second level of reality is that of patterns, which is the level of the mind. Thus the second body is termed the mental body. It is also called the astral body because of the association of astrology, as the astrological influence of the planets is one of patterning. It may also be called the *dream body*, because dreams often reflect mental patterns that are about to manifest physically.

Cayce also called the mental body the *emotional body*, for two reasons. The first is because Cayce was a forerunner of what today is called a "cognitive" theorist of emotion. Simply stated, it is the belief that emotions are secondary reactions, the primary reaction being cognitions, or ideas. We respond emotionally to situations on the basis of how we interpret them. If we interpret a situation using a threatening pattern to organize the data, we get scared—this will hurt me! Traditionally, psychology employed an instinctual, and then a physical conditioning approach to understanding emotions; contemporary psychology, however, has adopted a cognitive approach. The role of the instincts is seen as one of patterning. The physical basis of emotions, including their conditioning, is now understood to be based on a foundation of cognition. In other words, it's how you look at things that counts.

The second reason Cayce called the mental body the emotional body is because he saw a correspondence in the physical body itself between the three minds and the three bodies. In *psychic anatomy,* and in the realm of the psychic imagination, correspondences are the coin of the realm. Everything relates to patterns of vibration, octaves, and harmonics. Like the Jeweled Net of Indra, each point in the system reflects every other point. If there are three bodies, we will also find a reflection of all three in each one.

*Physical Body.* Cayce saw the operation of the superconscious mind and the soul body reflected and functioning in the endocrine system. The subconscious mind and the mental/emotional/astral body function and are reflected in the physical body through the autonomic nervous system. Finally, the conscious mind and the physical body are reflected by and operate through the cerebral-spinal system.

The cerebral-spinal system includes the sensory system and the voluntary nervous system, which control our muscles. To the average conscious mind, the cerebral-spinal system pretty much defines the real world, the sensory-material world that we can interact with consciously.

The autonomic nervous system is composed of the sympathetic and parasympathetic nervous systems, which control the functioning of our bodily organs. This system also is responsible for the physical effects of emotion: the sympathetic nervous system speeds up the heart under conditions of fear, while the parasympathetic system slows the heart during relaxation. Not only does this system operate outside of conscious awareness, it operates through the consciousness of the subconscious mind. Subliminal stimulation, for example, can excite the sympathetic nervous system through the medium of the subconscious mind without the conscious mind noticing the effects. Thus Cayce's designation for that body that corresponds to the subconscious mind as the emotional body of the autonomic nervous system is therefore quite appropriate.

From our traditional way of looking at anatomy, Cayce made a strange correlation when he linked the superconscious mind to the endocrine system. This linkage, however, is crucial to our understanding of the nature of psychic energies, and how our conscious and subconscious mind can influence the operation of these energies.

## THE CRYSTALLINE ENDOCRINE SYSTEM: PSYCHIC ENERGY TRANSDUCERS

How do the patterns of vibration of the fourth dimension—thoughts, ideas, and images—interact with the brain and the body of the three-dimensional world? How do the infinite and the finite interact? Recall our earlier discussion of how ideas "get into our head." Mental vibrations can "reach" from one person to the next because they transcend time and space. The brain resonates to vibrations. It can translate vibrations of the fourth dimension into activities going on with the body, and it can also do the reverse. For example, when one person picks up another person's emotional state, the emotions are visceral, gut reactions of the body; yet they are transmitted, one subconscious to another, by way of vibrations of the fourth dimension. How is this accomplished?

You may recall the old crystal radio sets. Through what seemed like a magical process that scientists call the "piezoelectric effect," the crystal can transform the electromagnetic vibrations of radio waves into the physical vibrations of sound. We have such a transformer in our body, an interconnected system of crystals known as the endocrine system.

The word *crystal* is more than merely an apt metaphor. The endocrine system functions like a system of crystal transducers, an electrical engineering term for a component that transforms energy from one form to another. Moreover, the physical evolution and operation of the endocrine system is related to that of crystals found in nature. In Cayce's story of creation, the souls' journey into the creation of bodies corresponded to the earth's formation, from a gaseous event into a solid planet. Crystals were formed within the depths of the earth by a process of solidification and precipitation. As souls were swimming within this cosmic brew, developing their sensory systems and their bodies, they projected their psychic energies into the developing crystals. As a result, the evolution of the body's endocrine system became a collateral development of the earth's crystalline deposits. In this way, the endocrine system corresponds to the earth's crystals. The soul's body and the earth are highly interdependent, historically and functionally.

Today there is much interest in the use of crystals for

healing and psychic development. The interest is appropriate, as it expresses the recollection of this primordial association of crystals with the "cross-over point," the interface between the sensory world of three dimensions and the underlying infinite world of the soul's psychic reality. What happens at the crossover, according to Cayce, happens at the level of what he calls the "rotary forces" of the atoms within the body. Quantum physics has discovered, if you recall, that a telepathic effect among atomic particles is expressed through their rotary action. It is here that the patterns of psychic energy and patterns of physical processes become one.

## THE CHAKRA SYSTEM AND KUNDALINI ENERGY

Cayce's description of the significance of the endocrine system for processing psychic energies was suggestive of the ancient yogic conception of kundalini energy and the chakras, or spiritual centers of the body. *Chakra* is a Sanskrit word meaning "wheel," or "wheel of force." Within each wheel, a certain kind of vital energy is stored. Cayce affirmed this resemblance. Thus, on the physical plane, there is the endocrine system, and on the psychic or spiritual plane there is the chakra system: two aspects of one reality.

In *Foundations of Tibetan Mysticism,* Lama Govinda also portrays the chakras as crystals, and describes them as the meeting point between spiritual energy and physical energy. Just as the body has three levels of reality—the soul body, the astral body, and the physical body—so does energy have its three levels. Again, Cayce reminds us first that all the energies are as one, yet can be experienced in earth as being of three types. The spiritual metaphysics of the East have their terms for these energies, as does Cayce. At the most basic level, corresponding to the level of pure spirit, is the *prana* energy. At the other end is the *kundalini* energy, which is also referred to as the "coiled serpent" or primal earth energy. There is also the energy that relates to the acupuncture channels in the body.

Each chakra has its own "seed sound." Focusing attention on the area of that chakra, visualizing it, and chanting its seed sound will open that chakra, releasing its energy. Psychic abilities and phenomena are associated with the opening of the chakras. Lama Govinda mentions that there are various Tibetan and Tantric exercises for opening the chakras in a constructive manner, since they are like Pandora's boxes of raw energy that can open for weal or woe. He mentions that much secrecy surrounds the methodology for working with chakras because of their volatile powers, which he likens to nuclear energy.

## KUNDALINI CRISES AND SPIRITUAL EMERGENCIES

A number of people sought readings from Edgar Cayce because they were having strange experiences: headaches with visions, energy sensations in the body, flashes of past-life recollections at odd moments, tremblings, bizarre and uncontrollable psychic experiences. He often described these events as the result of imbalances in the body corresponding to disturbances in the chakra system. Accidents, strong emotional reactions, improper meditation practices, headstrong and one-sided attempts to develop psychic abilities were among some of the causes Cayce gave for the imbalance in the flow of the kundalini energy. He noted also, in cases of "possession" or involuntary contact with entities, that when chakras are prodded open, they allow the energies from other subconscious minds to filter into a person's own energy system in a manner that would not otherwise occur. As the transducers of psychic energy, properly functioning chakras operate not only as psychic communicators, but also as a shield against unwanted communication. Cayce, and others since, have noted that the use of drugs and alcohol can produce "holes in the aura" that correspond to vulnerabilities in the etheric body due to improperly functioning chakras. These invite invasion from outside influences.

Here we have a host of examples of what Lama Govinda meant by the opening of Pandora's box! From descriptions such as Gopi Krishna's *The Awakening of Kundalini,* it is clear that even under experienced guidance the awakening of this energy can be quite a roller-coaster ride. Imagine the consequences when the energy is awakened in a haphazard manner.

Such crises in kundalini awakenings continue to this day, and in even greater numbers. The files at the A.R.E. are full of letters from people complaining of phenomena like those diagnosed by Cayce when he was alive. Such crises have become so commonplace that there is a subspecialty within clinical spiritual psychology for dealing with what is termed "spiritual emergencies." Prominent in this work are Stanislov and Christina Grof, who helped begin the Spiritual Emergency Network. In their work, they have found that kundalini crises can mimic any of the known psychiatric disorders. Traditional psychiatry tends to use medication for the treatment of these crises, but the practitioners in this new network have evolved an alternative system of treatment aimed at helping the person integrate the energies that have been released, while also attempting to stabilize the chakra system. As Cayce advised, these emergencies can then be taken as opportunities for growth, to become, in the terminology of the network, experiences of spiritual "emergence."

Anyone who has witnessed a person who is going through such an emergency can testify that opening the chakras is truly a powerful event. Clearly, working with these psychic energies should not be attempted lightly. It should be a matter of respect, as advocated by the masters. Cayce understood the inherent dangers, and tried to help us in this area by pointing to a foundation of wisdom for attuning to the chakras in a constructive manner.

# THE BOOK OF REVELATION: THE BIBLICAL THEORY OF THE CHAKRAS

In the ancient spiritual traditions of the East, the workings of the kundalini energy through the opening of the chakras was a highly valued and guarded secret. This energy is the key to the "fountain of youth," or the power of rejuvenation, the basic creative energies of life as manifested in a human body. It is here that the meeting of the Creator and the human being occurs in all its magical wonder.

If this knowledge has existed in the East for so long, why has not the Western world also had this knowledge? We have had it, indicates Cayce, but because of the extroverted attitude of the Western mind, we failed to notice the secret wisdom under our nose all along. He indicates that there is a systematic correspondence between the chakras and the endocrine system. His vision of the chakra system is drawn from a surprising source: the Bible.

While in a psychic trance, Cayce remarked that he could give much valuable information, if he were only asked, about the Book of Revelation, the last book in the New Testament. This comment caught the attention of his colleagues, who proceeded to work with Cayce on a detailed psychic study of this enigmatic chapter in the Bible. This group of people came to be called the Glad Helpers, for their principal focus has been healing through meditation and prayer. The work of this group, which continues today, is based largely upon their personal experience of the meaning of Revelation. The real "book of revelation" and its interpretation, Cayce stressed, is within each of our own bodies, where it waits to be opened and applied. The concepts that I present here primarily outline Cayce's orientation on the awakening of the psychic centers.

Cayce said that the Book of Revelation, believed to have been written by the apostle John, is a record of John's experience of cosmic consciousness—a kundalini awakening that John experienced within his own body.

## Symbology of the psychic centers

| Chakra | Endocrine gland | Church in the Revelation | Phrases from the Lord's Prayer |
|---|---|---|---|
| 1) Root | Gonads | Ephesus | "Give us this day our daily bread . . ." |
| 2) Water | Cells of Leydig | Smyrna | "Lead us not into temptation . . ." |
| 3) Solar Plexus | Adrenals | Pergamos | "Forgive us our debts . . ." |
| 4) Heart | Thymus | Thyatira | "In earth as it is in heaven . . ." "Deliver us from evil . . ." |
| 5) Throat | Thyroid | Sardis | "Thy kingdom come; Thy will be done . . ." |
| 6) Third Eye | Pineal | Philadelphia | "Hallowed be Thy name . . ." "And the power . . ." |
| 7) Crown | Pituitary | Laodicea | "Our Father, who art in heaven . . ." "And the glory, forever . . ." |

During this experience, his overself—the superconscious mind, or the Christ consciousness—instructs John as to the meaning of the experience and asks him to take responsibility for the knowledge revealed. The imagery in this book is thus a detailed account of what happens when the psychic centers are opened and what must be done in order to maintain mastery over the spiritual body. It is in this context that Cayce identifies the endocrine system as the "body" of the superconscious mind.

The number seven appears several times. This number corresponds to the seven glands of the endocrine system and the seven psychic centers, or chakras. The seven "churches" are the glands, while the seven "seals" are the chakras yet to be opened. The chart above provides a diagram of the correspondences between the individual glands, the psychic centers, and the symbology in Revelation.

The Book of Revelation, according to Cayce, does more than portray the anatomy of the endocrine system as the soul body of the superconscious mind. The instructions John received during his experience also explain how to become the master of this system, and thus the master of the body and the inheritor of the soul's legacy as a companion of God. When the emotions are calmed, like a "sea of glass," the four "beasts" of our lower nature come into harmony with the higher consciousness. When the cerebral-spinal nervous system, the "four and twenty elders," or cranial nerves, "bow down," or are quieted, the five senses cease their domination of consciousness so that the superconscious mind may rule. At this point, the "seals," or psychic centers can be opened. But by whom? "No man in heaven" can "open the book," but only the Christ consciousness, the "Root of David," is capable of opening the seals, upon the sacrifice of the self, or the consciousness of separation. There follows a description of the opening of the seven seals, and within each there is released an energy that is capable of being used for good or ill.

The drama of the events surrounding the opening of the seals is reminiscent of Lama Govinda's view that the opening of the chakras is like the opening of Pandora's box, something that must be done carefully, under the guidance of an experienced master following established spiritual patterns. The Book of Revelation provides a pattern of intelligence for the opening of the seals. Cayce concluded that the supreme pattern of awakening of the psychic centers was that of the Christ consciousness.

In the gospel according to Matthew, Jesus gave the people a prayer, the "Lord's prayer." In his psychic trance, Cayce indicated that this prayer was a patterning of the opening of the seven psychic centers and the circulation of those energies through the body. Like the Eastern tradition, it involves a pattern that places the higher centers in charge of the opening of the entire system. The correspondence Cayce perceived between

the lines in the Lord's prayer and the awakening of the
kundalini energy is shown in the chart on page 186.

The energy begins at the crown chakra ("Our Father,
Who art in Heaven") because the pituitary is the master
gland influencing all the others. Beginning here puts the
superconscious mind in charge of the activation of the
chakra system. The prayer proceeds down through
the pineal ("Hallowed be Thy name") and the thyroid,
or the will center ("Thy Kingdom come; Thy will be
done"), involving the sacrifice or "death" of the individual, separatist will of the conscious mind. The phrase
"On earth as it is in Heaven" refers to the harmony in
action of the upper and lower centers, and of the superconscious and the conscious levels. It corresponds to the
heart center, the thymus, which is often seen as the in-
termediating center between the upper and lower centers. At this point, the prayer moves down to the root
chakra ("Give us this day our daily bread") and then
shifts focus to calm the adrenals ("Forgive us our
debts"). Anxiety and fear are eliminated before continuing on to the cells of Leydig, the center of creativity
("Lead us not into temptation") in order to avoid the
temptation to squander or misapply creative energy.
The energy then begins its path upward to the higher
centers. Beginning with the heart center ("Deliver us
from evil"), and continuing on up, it culminates at the
crown chakra. The cycle can be repeated, again and
again as the energy circulates, transforming more and
more cells in the body.

Here are the essential characteristics of the pattern
Cayce recommended for the integrated opening of the
psychic centers. First, no one chakra is opened in isolation, but the entire system is activated holistically. Second, the activation of the chakras begins and is under
the control of the higher centers. Third, a cycle of activation is created, corresponding to the "circulation of
the light" described in the *Secret of the Golden Flower.*
Fourth, the lower chakras are not necessarily opened
sequentially, as it is important that the adrenals be calm
before the cells of Leydig are activated. Cayce indicated
that there is a triangle of energy, with the pineal and the

cells of Leydig acting as poles, and the solar plexus spreading that polar energy throughout the body. Opening the chakras in a context of fear or anger was thought to be more dangerous than opening them in a context of sexual excitement. Finally, the overall theme of the prayer is to put the energies into the service of the superconscious mind, rather than for personal exploitation. Psychic development achieved through a power motive typically creates fear as its other component. The prayer is focused on a serene state of mind based upon voluntary surrender to a higher power.

Cayce stressed that this prayer is definitely *not* the only way to work with the kundalini energies. It should not be used in a rote manner, he advised, but only if you can really feel the correspondences and find them meaningful. This is one example of an ideal pattern, based on the Christ consciousness.

I am fully aware of the controversial nature of these concepts. To the traditional Christian, the Book of Revelation is a prophecy of events to come. Cayce believed it to be prophetic, not of external events, but of inner experiences that await everyone as they come into awareness of the Christ consciousness. Because of the law of correspondence, however, the possibility cannot be dismissed that as more and more people come to experience the Christ consciousness, it will manifest in an external, historical upheaval that will also reflect the events in the Book of Revelation. On the other hand, many modern thinkers consider anything biblical antiquated material, and shy away from its consideration. Theirs is a conditioned response to its having been presented as literal fact by more fundamentalist Christians.

Carl Jung, however, came to a conclusion similar to that of Cayce. In *Answer to Job,* he points to a wide array of symbolism in Revelation that is not from the Christian tradition, but from other traditions, including paganism! Jung concludes that Revelation is a symbolic portrait of a universal, archetypal experience of the Self, which, as Jung believed, is equivalent to the Christ consciousness. Cayce often suggested the study of comparative religion as a means of better understanding the wider context of the novel interpretations he was giving. Jung's work, from the perspective of such a comparative study of the world's symbolism, is a case in point.

In any case, Cayce's description of the functioning of the endocrine system has proved so prophetic when compared with the recent discoveries of medical science, especially of the role of the endocrine glands and the immune system, that it deserves our attention.

## CAYCE IN MODERN TONGUE: PSYCHONEUROIMMUNOLOGY

Cayce's vision of the endocrine system came far in advance of science's more recent understanding of the glands. Cayce stressed the importance of treating the glands as a *system*. In fact, he called the endocrine system a nervous system that paralleled the more familiar one. Whenever he referred to the glandular system, he always mentioned the nerve bundles associated with them.

As modern neurophysiology learns more about the intimate connection between the endocrine system and the nervous system, it does seem as though the endocrine system is a parallel nervous system. The interconnections are complex. The endocrine glands secrete hormones into the blood system. Through the blood system, all organs of the body are affected, as is the chemistry of the brain. Various parts of the brain secrete hormones. The brain also sends nerve signals to the glands. For example, Cayce described how the Leydig interacted with the pineal, as a major activating system. Modern research has found that when the pineal is stimulated with light, the melatonin it secretes inhibits the Leydig's sex hormone production. Thus there becomes a feedback loop, making the endocrine system and the nervous system extremely interdependent.

The importance of the immune system to the body has focused much medical research on the complex functioning of the endocrine system. The thymus has been found to be responsible for the production of lymphocytes, the blood's major disease fighter (note that the thymus corresponds to "Deliver us from evil"). Many psychological factors that relate to "having heart," or becoming "downhearted," have been discovered to affect the thymus gland's ability to keep the immune system active. Such findings have led to the field of "psychoneuroimmunology," which is concerned with the interactive relationship of psychological factors, the nervous system, and the immune system. Here Cayce's complex view on the relationship between the mind and the body has begun to receive its most overall scientific support.

## ATTITUDES AND EMOTIONS: THE BODY'S NATURAL DRUGS

How did Cayce envision the influence of the body on psychic awareness? He stressed the impact of our emotional state upon bodily functioning and health. Attitudes are like chronic, or stable, emotional frames of mind. Together, our emotions and attitudes are like drugs in the body.

Our attitudes and emotions can poison us or make us "high." On the high side, the discovery of the brain's production of endorphins, a natural euphoriant, has led to a number of additional discoveries concerning how vigorous exercise, and such emotional responses as being in love, can stimulate the production of endorphins. Endorphins and other emotionally triggered chemicals have an effect on the endocrine system, and thus on psychic awareness.

Our language has long reflected this secret understanding of the relationship between emotions and bodily processes. We say that someone's behavior "galls" us, as if we knew that the effect of our emotional reaction was to increase bile secretion in the gall bladder. When we say, "I can't stomach that," we express our knowledge that our emotional reaction is upsetting the digestive system. The language of the emotions is full of such phrases that implicate the body. When a

person is in a chronic state of emotional arousal—
lonely, depressed, or resentful—the chemical effects begin to cause physical deterioration. Ulcers, headaches,
psoriasis, colitis, even allergies and cancer—these are
but a few of the syndromes that came to populate the
developing field of "psychosomatic" medicine that
Cayce had previsioned.

## TAKING RESPONSIBILITY FOR THE EMOTIONAL BODY OF ATTITUDES

Cayce, an activist who didn't think anyone need take it
lying down when their bodies became ill, anticipated the
modern perspective on "victim" psychology and advocated that people take responsibility for self-healing. In
particular, he maintained that a person could improve
the biological functioning of the body through meditation, which would calm the three bodies, and through
working to improve one's emotional attitudes. He also
extended this approach to the tuning of the body for
psychic awareness.

Clinical science has also validated Cayce's holistic
viewpoint with the discovery of biofeedback, with which
a person can learn to control the subconscious mind's
response to events and to how the subconscious mind
affected the autonomic nervous system it controlled.
Around the time of these exciting discoveries, meditation was becoming popular in the United States, and
clinical research found that it produced a number of
physical effects that had a positive impact upon the
body. Biofeedback and meditation began to enter the
medical vocabulary as techniques people could use to
contribute to their own healing. Voluntary control over
the so-called involuntary nervous system meant that it
was possible to communicate with the subconscious
mind. No longer did we have to remain victims of the
emotional body.

Treating the emotional body directly, as advocated by
Cayce, became headline news when Norman Cousins
revealed that he had healed himself of what the doctors

called a terminal malady by watching and enjoying many, many old comedy films. He noted that a good belly laugh was an effective anesthetic and showed positive effect on his endocrine system. Not only did Cousins's self-healing confirm Cayce's view that "laughter is the best medicine," it brought into focus the potential of shaping attitudes and emotions for the purpose of healing.

Soon research studies began to link attitudes and emotions to the chances of a person becoming ill, to the rate of recovery, and to specific effects upon the activity of the immune system. Ian Wickram, of the Eastern Virginia Medical School, developed a profile of proneness to psychosomatic illness. According to the profile, people who tend to worry, to perceive the world in terms of catastrophic expectations, and to dwell on negative memories are more likely to develop the type of overactive autonomic nervous system (the "emotional" body) that leads to psychosomatic distress. Bernard S. Siegel, author of Love, Medicine & Miracles, is a prime spokesman for the vast array of studies showing how the development of attitudes such as optimism and love are crucial to healing and recovery. Such general demographic findings have also been supported by research on the underlying causative mechanisms within the immune system itself. Depressions and loneliness weaken the immune system. Laughter, hopefulness, and feelings of love strengthen it. We now find Cayce's general principle of attitudinal health echoed in the words of holistic physician Norman Shealy, who says that the best antidote to stress and illness is to have "a positive, great attitude."

## THE PSYCHOKINETIC EFFECT OF BODILY IMAGERY

In attributing to the mind the ability to have specific control over the workings of the body Cayce especially anticipated the developments in modern medicine. Good attitude and positive emotions can be translated into specific instructions to the body. As we have seen, one way to communicate with the subconscious mind and the emotional body is through imagery. Dramatic effects attributed to imagery have been measured in the immune system. Through imagery, the mind can achieve quite effective control over the functioning of the cells in the immune system.

In *Imagery in Healing,* Jeanne Achterberg shows how this control can be so specific as to suggest a direct mind-to-body link. For example, scientists at Michigan State University showed their subjects slides of a particular type of cell and described its activities and attributes. They then asked them to attempt to visualize these cells leaving or entering the blood system. They found that their subjects were able to reduce or increase the count of these cells without affecting the other types of cells. In another experiment, they asked the subjects to attempt to change the extent to which these cells clung to the walls of the blood vessels. Again, the subjects were successful, being able to increase or decrease these cells' adherence factor at will. Although it is a somewhat thorny issue to invoke the concept of psychokinesis when the mind and the body belong to the same person, the degree of specific control of imagery over cellular production and function certainly seems magical.

Genuine psychokinetic effects have been achieved, however. William Braud, of the Mind Science Foundation in San Antonio, Texas, tested the ability of people to "mentally operate" upon the blood of another person. In one experiment, he found that the operator could affect the rate at which the red cells in drawn blood would break down. As of this writing, he is attempting to determine if people can affect processes within their own drawn blood. If they can, then there may be some basis for the general psychic notion that our minds affect our bodies through psychokinesis.

Cayce's belief in the creative power of the imagination to pattern physical manifestations is confirmed in the kind of bodily control that can be achieved through imagery. With regard to the psychic centers, therefore, it is understandable that Cayce would have stressed using visualization with extreme care if the centers are to be opened in a harmonious pattern.

## GROOMING THE PSYCHIC CENTERS

It is not necessary to open the psychic centers to manifest psychic awareness. They function as psychic receptors naturally. From Cayce's perspective, psychic functioning is an attribute of healthy, creative functioning which can be cultivated, if one desires, to include meditation for maximal development. It is always important to cultivate a healthy body, but especially if one is to attempt to meditate upon the psychic centers. Good grooming habits for the psychic centers will include not only physical, but mental, emotional, and spiritual habits as well—all have their effect upon the superconscious mind and its soul body, the endocrine system.

Cayce's suggestions regarding good physical habits are common sense by today's health-conscious standards. For example, the diet should be high in vegetables and low in red meat. Cayce would have us recognize that when we eat, we are incorporating life forms into our body, and they deserve our blessings. He also recommended periodic chiropractic adjustments to make sure that the spinal cord is not blocking the flow of vital energies.

A healthy body requires a healthy emotional frame of mind. Fearfulness, chronic anger, depression, and being under constant stress have a negative effect at all levels. Cayce's perspective on treating these problems is in line with the developing trend in holistic thinking. Dietary factors, such as coffee, sugar, and alcohol, can play a role in worsening the emotional and physical responses to stress. The current view in the field of psychological counseling is to examine patterns of thought, as advocated by Cayce. The types of thinking patterns he suggested be examined are much like those favored by current spiritually oriented psychologies, such as *A*

*Course in Miracles:* that we create our own psychological
realities, that the illusion of a separate self breeds fear,
anger, and addictions to power, suffering, relationships,
or material substances. In this perspective, meditation is
a major curative tool. We can use it not only as a calm-
ative, but also to facilitate self-acceptance and receptivity to feelings of Oneness with life.

It is worth noting that several of the alternative therapeutic modalities that Cayce referred to are now being
explored and have received some support in research
studies. In particular, the use of color, music, and odors
have been found to have both physical and psychological impact. Of these three, Cayce said that odor has the
most powerful influence, and his theory is gaining some
validation.

Gary Schwartz, for example, a well-known biofeedback researcher at Yale University, has begun research
on what he calls "aroma therapy." In one of his first
experiments he has found that the scent of spiced apples
lowers the blood pressure of a person who is emotionally upset. He has found that most of the scents that he
has studied have specific effects, including pain reduc-
tion (peaches) and easing hunger (chocolate). Psychiatrist Robert Turfboer, of Joplin, Missouri, has found
that burning scented matches eases insomnia. It should
also be noted that the sensation of inexplicable smells
sometimes accompanies psychic experiences. Studies
have indicated that approximately 8 percent of all experiences involving apparitions include an anomalous
smell, but smells may occur in other forms of psychic
experiences as well. When psychics were asked, "Do you
ever smell something when there is nothing to smell?"
Vernon Michael Neppe, of the University of the Witwa-
tersrand in Johannesburg, South Africa, found that they
all answered positively. A group of nonpsychics all answered in the negative. Among the psychics, the smells
were most often encountered in "the presence of an
entity," but also during mystical states and healing sessions.

Such findings bring into focus something of Cayce's
general philosophy of life, directed to healthy and happy

living within a context of a spiritual outlook, that has definite implications for the resultant development of psychic ability. In the words of Kevin Ryerson, a contemporary psychic channel who contributed to *Psychoimmunity and the Healing Process* (which contains much advice that parallels the suggestions in the Cayce readings), "It is more difficult to open the kundalini than to know God; and God is simply love. For love is that which unites all the chakras."

A person needn't perform spiritual calisthenics in order to develop psychic abilities. Many of the ordinary things that we do and think about have implications for the psychic centers. We can develop a healthy, happy life, knowing that by doing so, we are taking care of our physical, emotional, and soul bodies, promoting a natural development of psychic awareness.

What do you think about during the day? What do you read? What do you watch on TV? What we feed our subconscious through these activities, Cayce advised, has implications for the psychic centers. For example, it was found that watching a movie concerning Nazi war crimes depressed the immune system, while watching a movie about Mother Teresa strengthened it. In this day and age, when the stresses of life tire the adrenal glands, we get a surge of adrenaline energy from seeing the good guys go after the bad. But it is important to remember that psychic development in the context of an overactive solar plexus leads to unwanted psychic effects.

It would be better to give the adrenals a rest and to activate the higher centers by watching a restful movie, with soothing music, having some celestial scents in the room, fruits for a snack, and sharing all these delights with someone you love. In this very pleasurable manner, not only can you relax from the cares of the world, but you can be assured that you are grooming your psychic centers for optimal performance. In such an atmosphere, the body of the soul can rekindle its juices and perhaps urge you on to further adventure into psychic awareness.

# Part IV

# DEVELOPING PSYCHIC AWARENESS

# 11
# ADVENTURE INTO PSYCHIC AWARENESS

*First, begin between selves. Set a definite time, and each at that moment put down what the other is doing. Do this for twenty days. And ye will find ye have the key to telepathy.*

EDGAR CAYCE reading no. 2533–7

DON'T TAKE ANYBODY'S WORD for it. Try it for yourself and see. You'll learn more secrets by your own experiments and practice than just by thinking about the theory. Besides, only the ideas that actually work for you, those you use and that *make a difference in your life,* are worth anything, anyway." Such would be Edgar Cayce's advice on becoming psychic. Enlightenment doesn't come just by sitting quietly, but by enlightened action that bears the fruit of knowledge.

What kind of enlightened action can you take? In addition to the specific suggestions given in the preceding chapters, you may wish to try some additional experiments during your adventure in psychic awareness.

By now you have learned that you are one with the world. By now you may believe in the possibility of ESP, which helps develop psychic ability. Allow your imagination to embrace concepts that transcend space, time, and the cause-and-effect chain of atomistic thinking. Imagine ideas as permeating the fourth dimension and allow your own mind to become a sympathetic resonator to these patterns. Imagine that behind the veil of your conscious awareness there exists a superconscious intelligent awareness. Develop your own image of this intelligence at work, this Ancient One within you who is guiding you *at this moment* in your very next step.

## PREPARE A PLAN OF APPLICATION

What will you do with your psychic ability? If you have no plan for using it, you may feel overwhelmed and afraid. Prepare in advance by thinking about how you could use psychic ability, and then get ready to do so. Trying to develop ESP out of curiosity alone will not be sufficient, in the long run, to bring out your psychic ability. You need to create experiments that have a practical application to an area of personal need.

Get ready to use your psychic ability to overcome obstacles and further develop and express your talents. You might also use it to help other people, to bring goodness into the world. Develop an agenda based on your needs or on specific purposes for putting psychic awareness in action. It will help you focus your energy as you experiment with the various techniques for developing ESP.

If you are frustrated at work and wish you could get a fresh start in a new career, for example, psychic ability may help you make that move. You may become aware of hidden talents or locate training or employment opportunities. Psychic ability might give you the added resources you need to go into business for yourself, matching your talents with the needs of the marketplace.

Develop some specific goals you wish to work for and accomplish, that you are now prepared to implement. Give your intentions to develop ESP some practical motivation. When you are ready to have the winds blow, then raise your sail and get your hand on the rudder. Be prepared!

# DREAM RECORDING FOR SYNCHRONISTIC PATTERN

Chances are your first psychic experience will occur in a dream. Don't miss out. During the day, ask yourself if you are prepared to remember a psychic dream. As you go to sleep at night, imagine yourself waking up in the morning with a helpful dream. Prepare yourself to dream psychically. Get a dream journal and begin writing in it each morning, even if it is simply to record your impressions and thoughts upon awakening. Dipping into the back of your mind to locate almost forgotten dream memories is good practice for keeping in contact with the subconscious mind. The transitional state upon waking is a prime moment to receive psychic impressions.

During the day, be on the lookout for patterns of correspondence between your dreams, or waking impressions, and the day's experiences. Don't be too rational about evaluating any perceived correspondences. If you sense a link, assume there is one. The proof comes not in the analysis, but what happens next when you follow it up.

Look at correspondences as possible opportunities to put your psychic awareness into application. Suppose, for example, you are prepared to use psychic ability to help you move into a new career. You have a dream of playing with children and the next day you see a TV news spot on the needs of underprivileged children that shows an adult accompanying a child at the playground. There's a correspondence. Might it be pointing to an opportunity to move into a career involving children? Might it be pointing to an opportunity that awaits you if you become more childlike and playful? How can you test out these ideas? Going to a playground to relax and "mess around" for a few minutes might lead to a new idea, or a chance encounter with a stranger who may suggest the next step. Looking into the possibility of opening a daycare center for underprivileged children may lead you to discover a host of opportunities for work with children.

# SET YOURSELF ASIDE

You may not be ready to begin a program of meditation, even though you are aware of its supreme value in developing psychic awareness. That's perfectly okay. Applying your innate intuitive abilities before you begin any special program of development is a natural way to proceed. Meditation is a special case of learning to set aside the conscious mind in favor of superconscious awareness, but there are other ways to practice the art of letting go. Cayce suggested an exercise that is similar to what is called in the Eastern tradition "mindfulness meditation." You can use it as an aid to working with spontaneous intuition.

For brief periods of time, then for longer periods, try to stay in contact with your background awareness, then simply "step aside and watch yourself go by." That is, without interfering with or changing any of your thoughts and actions, simply observe them. At first, you may wish to practice repeating the phrase, "Now I am aware that I am . . ." thinking about this, or doing that, and so forth. The idea is to be able to combine awareness with spontaneity. We are usually able to have one or the other, but not both at the same time. Practicing this form of ongoing meditation will yield several useful benefits.

It is not possible to set self aside without first accepting yourself. You will learn self-acceptance by this exercise. You may have to become aware that, "Now I am blocking out feelings about . . ." or, "Now I am criticizing myself for . . .". Self-criticism inhibits curiosity, and has the effect of closing you rather than opening you to spontaneity.

As you practice this form of awareness, you can take an inventory of habitual thought patterns that interfere with the development of higher consciousness. Do you find that you are skeptical of your developing psychic awareness? Do you have patterns of worry, of fear, or of anger? Make a note of them. Later you can investigate these patterns to see how you might work with them.

Use inspirational writing, for example, to have a dialogue between the insecure you and your higher Self.

By taking an attentive, loving interest in those parts of you that you want to change, you will break the fruitless habit of thoughtless, automatic self-criticism and learn to recognize the various underlying needs that these parts are trying to bring to your attention. Knee-jerk self-criticism expresses both an addiction to "self"-perfection as well as underlying fears for the preservation of that separate "self." Learning to work with such patterns in an accepting rather than a controlling way builds self-confidence and dissolves the fears that will later block spontaneous psychic awareness.

Developing self-acceptance will enable spontaneous thoughts and urges, which you might have otherwise pushed away, to come to the surface. Responding to intuitions requires that you be sensitive to irrational promptings that may come in the form of images and feelings. If you want to express intuition, you need to learn that you can trust the flow of your experience.

## LEARNING TO TRUST YOUR INTUITION

You have to learn to trust your intuition, and this means learning to *act* on it. Cayce's yes/no intuition exercise, given earlier, is a good way to look to your intuition for advice. But you don't have to wait until you face an important decision. Your intuition is working all the time. Try acting on it.

Here is a simple suggestion to get started. Try to get in the habit of announcing who the caller is every time the phone rings. When you hear the phone ring, simply speak up and declare, "That is . . . calling," blurting out whatever name comes to you. Intuition is knowing without knowing how you know. So assume an "innocent-knowing" frame of mind, and make the announcement out loud, as if you really know who it is. If you feel hesitant, perhaps you can appreciate the results of research indicating that intuitive people are willing to take risks and are not afraid to expose themselves to criticism. So take a chance.

Take note of the results. When you are correct, note how your valid intuitions feel when they come. When you are incorrect, examine what was on your mind as you made your announcement. Perhaps you will discover that there was some thought or image connected with the person who was calling, something you suppressed or discounted. Those oversights will also teach you something of what the ingredients of intuition feel like.

Are you slow to make even the most trivial decisions? Try acting quickly and spontaneously, without much thought. Make quick choices about which movie to see or what to order from the menu, as a means of developing the intuitive response. I enjoy making predictions about how movies will turn out or the identity of the culprit in detective stories, which is another enjoyable way to turn everyday situations into intuition games.

Habit can stifle intuition, whether it be habits of daily routine, or those of rational thought. It can be helpful to juggle your daily routine to develop a flexibility that can more readily admit the promptings of intuition. Do you drive home from work the same way every day? Try varying the route. Try going for a random drive, and at each intersection make a spontaneous choice of direction.

Combine such experiments with your program of action for using your awakening psychic ability. As you go on a random drive, be sensitive for any inner promptings to pull over and investigate some business establishment—just to visit, perhaps—that might prove to relate to your finding a new direction for a career move.

You can also apply this approach to your dreams. Try assuming that your dreams are intuitive visions and act on them. Seek out or create experiences that correspond with your dream images. If you dream of a friend, call the person up for a chat. If you dream of riding your bike, go for a ride. Let any other intuitions that might arise while you are doing such things prompt spontaneous actions, questions, searchings. You may find yourself another step down the road to an opportunity for a new career. Working with your dreams in this intuitive way can be enhanced if you specifically attempt to "incubate" dreams, as described in chapter five, on specific applied topics of interest.

## EXPERIMENT WITH A PENDULUM

You can discover the psychic ability of your subconscious mind by working with a pendulum. After the pendulum has helped you by-pass your conscious mind and gain access to the ESP of your subconscious, you should gradually dispense with the pendulum and pick up messages from your subconscious directly. You may begin with an experiment that is done just for "curiosity," but then progress to something more in keeping with your plans for applying psychic ability.

The use of a pendulum in an ESP test has been found to produce more accurate results than guessing. Try to see if you can obtain this effect yourself. Have a friend sit down out of your sight, pick a card from a deck, and focus on the color red or black. Try to guess the color of the card. After each guess, have your friend show you the card so you can see it for yourself. Run through a series of ten cards and keep track of your score. Then switch to using a pendulum. Determine which pendulum response will represent black, and which will represent red. Run through a series of ten cards again, allowing the pendulum response to determine the guess. Switch back and forth between doing a run of ten cards by guessing and ten cards with the pendulum. At the end, see which was more accurate. If the pendulum was more accurate, you have evidence of how the pendulum can access your subconscious mind's psychic ability better than your conscious mind can.

By the way, getting eight or more out of ten right would definitely be considered as beating the odds. Getting only two or less right would be considered "negative ESP," meaning you are demonstrating ESP, but using it to make yourself wrong. If that is the case, perhaps ESP frightens you.

When you have satisfied yourself that the pendulum can demonstrate ESP in guessing cards, then try to wean yourself from it. Begin by seeing if you can guess in advance how the pendulum is going to respond. When you can do that without reducing the pendulum's ESP accuracy, then you are probably ready to dismiss the pendulum for card guessing.

Now try something that relates to your plan of application for using psychic abilities. Here's an idea concerning careers. Cut out some help wanted ads from your newspaper. Pick a few that relate to jobs you know you would really hate, and a few that you think you might like. In addition, pick about twice as many for jobs you aren't sure about. Paste each ad on a separate index card. Then take the pendulum and establish its response code. Perhaps left to right would mean, "I would *do well* in this job," while forward and backward would mean, "I would *not do well* in this job." And swinging in a clockwise circular pattern would mean "I would *like* this job," while swinging in a counterclockwise pattern would mean, "I would *not like* this job." No movement could indicate, "No opinion." The choice of responses should be based on the type of questions you are concerned with—career preferences, innate abilities, hunches that it would lead to something good, prospects of being hired and so forth. Once the pendulum response "code" is established, read each want ad in turn, and note your pendulum response. See if it corresponds with your conscious opinion. When it doesn't, try again. If the pendulum continues to give you a consistent response, but one that is different than your conscious opinion, you may have something to think about.

To test for ESP effects, have your friend pick one of these cards at random and silently read it while thinking about you in connection with such a job. Check your pendulum response to the job card now, when only your friend knows its identity. If the pendulum tends to make the same response to the job card whether you are looking at the card, or whether your friend is looking at it and you don't know the card's identity, you are getting some interesting ESP effects. Have your friend run through the cards a few times and find cards that your pendulum responds to in a consistent manner. Here is a very interesting ESP effect, one that can have some potential meaning for you in terms of career questions. These job cards must relate to careers to which your subconscious mind, for some reason, is very sensitive. Discuss your feelings about these jobs with your friend, including your friend's impressions of your abilities, preferences, and so forth, which your pendulum may have been picking up on. Follow up on the discussion, using dream incubation, inspirational writing, or the meditation "yes/no" experiment, described in previous chapters.

The primary value of the pendulum is its ability to demonstrate the ESP ability to your subconscious mind prior to your being able to experience psychic imagery. The pendulum should be recognized, however, for the automatism that it is. It would not be a tool favored by Cayce himself, because its use suggests opening oneself to outside influence. In comparison to automatic writing and the Ouija board, however, the pendulum allows only a limited degree of conscious dissociation; thus it is not particularly dangerous if you don't rely on it as a substitute for developing your own psychic awareness. The pendulum serves to amplify the reaction of your subconscious mind to make it visible to the eye. Having thus seen that your subconscious is responding psychically, you should be able to develop the mental equivalent of the pendulum by focusing on your feelings and imagery.

## MENTAL TELEPATHY: EXPERIMENTS IN REMOTE VIEWING

Cayce once suggested an experiment he said would demonstrate the key to telepathy: Arrange with a friend to set aside some time each day when both of you, each in your own particular location, can sit quietly and try to

tune in on the other person. Allow your mind to resonate with the other person's experience (thoughts, recent activities, feelings, surroundings, plans, and so
forth) and make notes or diagrams about what you pick
up. Check in with each other regularly and compare
notes. Cayce suggested trying this experiment for twenty
days in a row. You should see some results.

The merits of this approach to investigating telepathy
have been repeatedly validated. It was made famous by
Upton Sinclair, who worked with his wife over a long
period of time and wrote of their experiences in his
book *Mental Radio*. Harold Sherman (the psychic from
Arkansas who, with Ingo Swann, made the psychic trips
to Jupiter and Mercury described in chapter one), used
this approach to stay in telepathic contact with Sir Hu-
bert Wilkins on his exploration of Antarctica. Together
they wrote an account of their experiments in *Thoughts
Through Space*. René Warcollier, in *Mind to Mind*, reported the results of hundreds of such experiments and
outlined the ingredients of success.

The method has gained even greater popularity in
contemporary psychical research under a new name, *remote viewing*. First conducted at Stanford Research Institute (now SRI International) by Russell Targ and
Harold Putoff, remote-viewing experiments have become common, because of their apparent simplicity and
because most anyone seems able to quickly learn to do
it. In these experiments, an agent goes to some unknown location and surveys the scene. Meanwhile, back
at the lab, the viewer simply describes to an interviewer
whatever is going on in the viewer's mind and then
makes a diagram of any visual images. The viewer's report and diagrams are then compared with the scenes of
the location visited by the agent. Targ and Putoff describe many successful experiments in *Mind Reach* and
*The Mind Race*.

Such experiments have all shown that spontaneous
imagery is crucial to their success. Failure is often
caused by the rational mind altering the spontaneous
impressions based on expectations. Thus the experiments I suggested earlier, concerning learning to "set

self aside" and developing the spontaneity of intuition, are good training techniques for success at remote viewing.

## EXPERIMENTS IN CLAIRVOYANCE

Researchers at SRI International discovered that the same skills used in picking up on the experiences of a remote agent could also be used to pick up information even when there was no sending agent involved. For example, in one series of experiments described in *The Mind Race,* subjects were given a random set of latitude-longitude coordinates and they successfully "viewed" the scenery at these locations. In another series of experiments, subjects successfully "viewed" the contents of microdot documents—about the size of the dot on an "i"—sealed in containers.

Under the modern terminology of remote viewing, these workers successfully extended the range of typical clairvoyance. The tasks were no different than those performed by Edgar Cayce in his psychic trance, when he described what the person he was reading for was doing at the moment, and what the surroundings looked like, or when he peered microscopically into the workings of the person's body. Cayce's psychic source once indicated that he could be an even better clairvoyant in his waking state than in his trance state, if he wished to develop himself properly. The remote-viewing experiments seem to support at least the notion that a trance is not always necessary for psychic awareness. Another implication drawn by the researchers is that an extension of belief in what's possible actually extends the range of the possible. Here is another reminder to keep expanding the limits of your imagination.

In his waking state, Edgar Cayce could discern the contents of a letter simply by holding the sealed envelope. He often picked up additional information about the sender, almost as if he were giving a preview of the reading that would result from the person's request.

Cayce's waking ability can be adapted to some experiments for you to try.

Have a friend purchase a number of fine art picture postcards and seal each one in an opaque envelope. Take one of these envelopes into your hand and allow your mind to become one with the postcard, resonating to the picture. Accept your first impressions without censoring them, and note them down. Then open the envelope and compare your impressions with the picture. In your comparison, look for aspects of the picture that might relate to impressions that you suppressed. Don't try too many pictures in one sitting, and space your experiments out over several days or weeks. It might also be worthwhile to experiment with altered states of consciousness. Try sleeping on an envelope and see if your dream contains elements of the picture. Try taking advantage of the transitional period upon waking up in the morning to "view" the contents of an envelope. Try viewing an envelope during a session of relaxation or autohypnosis. It would also be useful to compare your skills before and after a period of meditation.

Think of a way to adapt this kind of experiment to the specific area of application you are interested in for developing your psychic ability. The career cards I described earlier could easily be substituted for the art cards. Hold an envelope with an unknown want ad inside, while allowing your mind to receive images spontaneously. In addition to testing your ESP in this way, it is also possible that a comparison of your mental imagery with the want ad could lead to some intuition about a previously unsuspected aspect of that kind of job.

## VIEWING THE FUTURE

Typical ESP experiments that require a subject to make repeated guesses among a limited set of options (such as, will the card be red or black?) tend to become boring. Cayce stressed the need to develop ESP experiments that challenge the person to accomplish something of practical value. Recently, researchers have combined these two considerations into an experimental approach that has tremendous potential. It is called "associative remote viewing of future events." One of the first researchers to attempt this type of study was Elizabeth Targ, whose experiment concerned the outcome of an election.

In the fall of 1980, the question was "Who will be elected president: Ronald Reagan, Jimmy Carter, John Anderson, or none of these men?" In this case, to ask for a psychic prediction is actually asking a person to guess among only four choices. Rather than asking for this kind of guess, Targ used a different approach. She asked a friend to secretly select four completely different objects of any sort and put each one in a box. The boxes were then to be randomly labeled "Reagan," "Carter," "Anderson," and "None of these." Tart then told the experimental subject—the "viewer"—that on the night of the election she would be shown an object. What would it be? The subject's task was not to guess "which one," for the choices were not known, but simply to allow imagery to arise spontaneously in her mind. Targ related the viewer's imagery to her friend, who was asked if it matched any of the objects. If it did, the bet was on. If it didn't, then it would be assumed that the subject had not been able to view the future. As it turned out, the subject's description, "a white, hollow, conical object . . . like shell material . . . with a string attached to its apex," clearly matched one of the objects the friend had gathered, a "cornucopia-shaped whistle made from an animal horn with a string attached to its pointed end." That object happened to be in the box labeled "Reagan." The election returns later proved the viewer had correctly predicted the outcome.

There was one more crucial part of this experiment. When the results of the election were known, Targ went to her friend, got the whistle, and showed it to the experimental subject. Since the experiment was based upon the assumption that the subject would be shown an object, this final act of following through seemed important. It's staggering to consider the implications for our typical way of thinking about time and causality: would the experiment have worked if Targ had forgotten about the final act of feedback? Did the act of showing the viewer the object retroactively *cause* the viewer to "see" that object eight weeks earlier?

In spite of this philosophical enigma, one aspect of the methodology that makes the approach so appealing is that since the viewer is faced with an open-ended situation, if the viewer correctly perceives one of the associated targets, it seems likely that accurate psychic functioning is involved. Associative remote viewing of future events has been profitably employed to make financial predictions. An organization of applied psychical forecasting, Delphi Associates, was formed by some of these researchers to extend this method to financial consulting. It has been quite successful. In fact, they were able to make tens of thousands of dollars on the silver futures market with this method. Whether used for financial speculation or some other purpose, if you have to make a decision about the outcome of a future event, you might considering creating an experiment along these lines.

From these experiments in associative remote viewing I reached the conclusion that a future event could affect my present functioning. I applied this idea while preparing to write this book. First, I went to a bookstore and found the shelf of books on psychic phenomena. Then I promised myself that after this book was published, I would go to the store and look at my book. I would look at the cover, the table of contents, and the layout of pages. I would also read selected passages, especially ones I had trouble writing. I let that commitment grow until I could feel it as a reality. Then, when I got stuck in my writing, I would lie down and use my self-hypnosis induction method to enter a state of reverie. I would then "travel" to the bookstore and look up my book. I found I could turn to the pages corresponding to my problem, and read how I had solved it. I would then get up and decide whether I liked that solution—I usually did—and implement it. I don't know if I was seeing the future or creating it, or if it was simply a way of inducing creative problem-solving imagery, but it got me through many an impasse in writing the book. To be on the safe side, however, I do plan to go to that bookstore to check out my predictive "visions"—just to ensure the presence of the crucial "cause" of my being able to "prophesy" the future.

I also imagine you shaking your head in disbelief, thinking, "He didn't prophesy his book's outcome, he wrote it that way!" Psychic awareness has its own logic; all I can suggest is that you judge the book, and my methods, by whether or not you've been helped through reading it.

## OPEN CHANNELING IN TRANCE

Using an altered state of consciousness to elicit imagery for creative problem solving is a good application for learning open channeling in trance. Robert Davé of Michigan State University, for example, studied people who were at an impasse in their creative work. He either suggested that they think more about it, or he hypnotized them and suggested they dream a solution for the problem. One week later, 75 percent of the people who had experienced a hypnotic dream had solved their creative problem, whereas only 12 percent of the thinkers had solved theirs. It's worth learning self-hypnosis, or autogenic training, to be able to experiment with such an approach to evoking inspiration.

Once the trance state has been mastered, enter it with a specific question addressed to your higher Self. Having asked the question, allow your mind to run freely. Be aware of thoughts that may whisper subtly. Accept any feeling of knowing that may exist. Be sensitive to any images that arise. Very often a solution comes in the form of a single image rather than an elaborate dream. That single image can be the intuition of your higher Self speaking in a very succinct manner.

This same method can be used for interpreting dreams. While in this trance state, have a friend read one of your dreams aloud to you. Then call upon the highest within you and allow yourself to speak about your dream. I have found that even novices can deliver quite meaningful discourses about their own dreams in this manner. Deep within us, we know the truth about ourselves. If we are willing to assume the responsibility for consciously knowing that truth, we can use this method to bring that knowledge into awareness. For this purpose, the trance state itself may prove to be less important than the attitude of acceptance.

## SENDING TELEPATHIC SUGGESTIONS

Have you ever wanted to send a telepathic message to someone to seek assistance? The early research we reviewed on hypnosis at a distance suggests the possibility. Psychics have admitted to this ability, but have been hesitant to use it.

In a rare gesture of mischieviousness, Edgar Cayce once made a bet to a friend that he could mentally induce a mutual acquaintance, someone who was extremely skeptical about Cayce's work, to come to Cayce and ask for a psychic reading. The proposition seemed improbable and the bet was on. The next day, the person in question appeared, hat in hand, at Cayce's studio asking for help. Afterward, Cayce vowed he would never do it again.

Al Miner, a professional psychic, told me of an instance when he used telepathic suggestion when working as a motor-home salesman. It worked the first time. The second time, however, the would-be customer called Al and said he developed such a strong urge to buy a motor-home that he bought one at the closest place available—another dealer. Chagrined, Al stopped using this technique.

In *Parapsychology and the Unconscious*, Jules Eisenbud argues that the unconscious use of telepathic suggestion to get our way with other people is probably universal. He notes, however, that the attempt to use it consciously creates a reactionary fear in most practitioners. One way to deal with unconscious tendencies is to attempt to channel them into positive applications. Cayce often reminded us that through our connection with one another at the subconscious level, our thoughts affect other people. He advises that we think only the best about others and pray for people who upset us.

My wife introduced me to a constructive application of telepathic suggestion that will lend itself to an experiment you can try yourself. When I had trouble falling asleep, she would pray for me and imagine me asleep. She said she was convinced that, if she didn't succumb to her own suggestion first, it worked on me. There are reasons to believe her. Cayce indicated that during the presleep state we are very susceptible to suggestion, as Cynthia Pike's *The Miracle of Suggestion: The Story of Jennifer* proves so true. Thomas Jay Hudson noted his successful experiments in sending telepathic suggestions of healing to distressed people while they slept. Eisenbud describes experiments in Russia that confirm the induction of hypnotic sleep by telepathic suggestion.

Many parents have children who have difficulty falling asleep. The current wisdom is that the sleep disturbance is a behavioral problem that is reinforced by parental attention. A recent television news-magazine program showed a psychologist training parents of a sleep-disturbed child to eliminate the problem. The technique was to go into the bedroom and comfort the child, but to delay doing so for progressively longer periods. Before a week was up, the behavioral reshaping had the desired result. If you have such a child, try this method first. If it doesn't work, consider an alternative. Try meditating and silently inviting your child to join in the silence. Whether through meditation, prayer, or the sending of telepathic suggestion while you are relaxed yourself, you may find your child following suit. Success at this experiment will mean your child will sleep peacefully but may cause you to lose some sleep wondering about the implications of this newfound telepathic ability.

# CRYSTALS AND GEMSTONES

An article in *Time Magazine*, January 19, 1987, spoofed the growing popularity of the use of crystals in the pursuit of New Age consciousness. Cayce, revealing how the earth's crystals were connected with the endocrine system of the soul's body, had recommended their use as an aid in attunement. He also indicated that, long ago, crystals and gemstones had been used in healing and that this knowledge would someday reappear. Current trends would suggest that at least the past enthusiasm, if not some of the knowledge, has resurfaced.

In his recommendations for the use of gemstones and crystals, Cayce suggested that some minerals are more effective for certain purposes than others. On the other hand, he reminded us that all energy is from the same source, and that it is within us. Thus the use of these minerals can only act as an aid and a support for our own efforts at attunement. Here is the approach to working with crystals and gemstones that I evolved from his philosophy. As he indicated, some of this methodology had to emerge from my own intuition.

I concluded that each mineral was best suited for holding, like a battery, or amplifying, like a resonator, a certain pattern of energy. For meditation and psychic awareness, Cayce usually recommended the copper-based minerals, such as azurite/malachite. I assumed that the power of attunement was not in the stone, but something to be developed within me. The value of the stone was in its ability to store the energy that came to me during meditation, and then, at other times, to make that accumulated energy available to me. Thus I would not meditate *on* the stone; rather, while holding the stone, I would allow it to resonate to my meditative energies. In this way, the stone "sponged" up and stored the energy and pattern of my attunement experiences.

I learned how to "listen" to the stone to hear its "tone," which I took to be the auditory image of its resonating pattern. Others may attune to minerals through visual imagery. I found confirmation of the use of auditory imagery in Native American traditions. Once I learned to "hear" the stone's tone, I assumed that the key to opening the stone was to resonate with it by my "sounding" its tone, either aloud or silently, thus releasing for my use all of the energy that I had accumulated within the stone.

Cayce suggests wearing stones and crystals on various parts of the body corresponding to the locations of the various chakras. It is worth experimenting, as many have, with various ESP tasks, and comparing the results obtained with and without the use of properly prepared stones. One of the experiments I conducted was to test the use of my tonal technique on the inner experience of a person who was holding my stone. While the person was in a distant location, or asleep, I would either silently sound the stone's tone, a different tone, or no tone. Comparing the person's report under these conditions convinced me of the potential value of learning to work with gemstones and crystals.

The use of crystals in laser holography has led to the development of new conceptual imagery for understanding consciousness and psychic awareness. The recent explosion of interest in the psychic use of crystals and gemstones may well mark the emergence of modern psychophysics—the intuitive recollection of knowledge from Atlantis, predicted by Cayce—whereby people, working in harmony with one another and with the natural elements, are able to meet their material needs through the use of transcendent psychic awareness.

# 12
# TRANSCENDENT PSI IN COMMUNITY

*For one human being to love another, that is the
ultimate, the last test and proof, the work for
which all other work is but a preparation.*

RAINER MARIA RILKE

**A HEADLINE IN THAT** staid financial daily *The
Wall Street Journal* on October 22, 1984, was startling:
"Did psychic powers give firm a killing in the silver market? And did greed ruin it all?" The article concerned
the experiments in remote viewing that we discussed in
the previous chapter. Russell Targ and his colleagues at
Delphi Associates had earned $120,000 predicting
fluctuations in the price of silver. Then, however, the
experiment went sour. Targ speculated that the prospects of great personal gain interfered with the ability to
stay gently focused on the psychic wavelength. Learning
this lesson led Targ to a new direction in his research.
He is now trying to determine the effect of motivation—
whether personal reward or spiritual purpose—on
psychic functioning. Thus the latest in psychical research confronts an age-old question: does psychic
awareness operate independently or as an aspect of
spirituality?

## SPIRITUALITY AND PSYCHIC AWARENESS

In the ancient yoga tradition it was common knowledge
that psychic powers developed as a result of intense

meditation. The same has been true in Western mysticism. In 1982, parapsychologist Rhea White surveyed the biographies of saints and found that 29 percent exhibited ESP. Spontaneously coming to a person's aid, bilocation (appearing to be in two places at once), and acquiring knowledge clairvoyantly were some of the examples she cited. The majority of these saints were not born psychic, she noted, but their skills increased with their spiritual work and progress.

Philosopher Michael Grosso argues that the extraordinary psi phenomena exhibited by spiritual devotees suggests something important about the nature of ESP. He notes how surveys of psi research show that ESP functioning is diminished when the subject is involved in "ego-involving efforts," but is enhanced by being able to let go of concerns for sensory world and for personal accomplishment. He identifies a "transcendent" mode of being, which supersedes a concern for personal survival, that is conducive to psi phenomena. This transcendent mode is similar to empathy. For example, to be a good listener, we must suspend our own frame of reference and our own concerns to be able momentarily to adopt the other person's perspective. He suggests that *love* is the essential attribute of that transcendent mode of being. Playfulness and an enjoyment of the process itself of doing things seem to be correlates of this self-transcendent state of mind.

Grosso does not equate spirituality with being "good" as opposed to being "bad" or "evil." There are no moral overtones to his proposition concerning what he terms *transcendent psi*. Spirituality seems to have more to do with being "smart," as in enlightened, rather than being "good," as in perfect. It is enlightened self-interest—in other words, smart—to act in accord with how things really are from a larger perspective, rather than how they might appear from a constricted viewpoint. Ecology, holography, quantum physics—all such developments in applied holistic thinking—are abandoning an atomistic viewpoint in favor of the Perennial Philosophy of the interconnectedness of life: Oneness. The essence of love, of altruism, of service to others—in effect, the essence of transcendence—is to act on the basis of a perception of Oneness, of an interdependent whole. That seems to be the emerging meaning of spirituality.

Cayce's view of the relationship of psychic awareness to spirituality is similarly oriented to this concept of the transcendent. Psychic awareness exists because, in reality, we are souls: interconnected miniature versions of the whole of creation, holographic atoms in the body of God. To become consciously psychic requires empathizing with the Oneness of life, rather than focusing on one's separate self. Attempting to use psychic awareness for personal gain is "sin" only in that it misses the mark and constricts the focus to the self. Psychic ability is an expression of the whole. It is designed to be used for the betterment of the whole, including, if necessary, improving our recognition and application of our unique contribution to the whole.

Cayce, aware of the paradox, quoted Jesus from Luke 9:24: "For whosoever will save his life shall lose it; but whosoever will lose his life for my sake, the same shall save it." To Cayce, and to Jung, the significance of Jesus is that he lived the pattern of an individual in conscious, creative, and responsible relationship to the whole. That pattern of self-realization, both an acceptance and a transcendence of the personal ego, exists as a potential for each of us. Psychic awareness can be seen both as an outgrowth and a means of attuning to that pattern of being.

## THE PARADOX OF RESEARCH ON TRANSCENDENT PSI

Grosso recommends that research on psychic phenomena be reoriented toward transcendent psi. He realizes that following this suggestion might meant using a different type of experiment than that ordinarily employed. The new wine requires that the old wineskin be laid aside. A paradox confronts most experiments in ESP that are approached from the traditional, atomistic standpoint. The experimenter designs a situation to see if the subject can demonstrate psychic ability. If you were the subject in such an experiment, it would be only natural to ask yourself, "Am I psychic?" The situation is inherently self-conscious, and self-consciousness inhibits psychic awareness.

Cayce refused to be a subject in an ESP experiment if the focus was to test his ability or to prove ESP. He wanted to cooperate with parapsychology, for he thought it was important to demonstrate the reality of Oneness. But he was convinced that it was impossible to attempt to prove it in a philosophical context of skepticism, because the focus of such an experiment would make it difficult to manifest psychic awareness. He maintained that the driving force of psychic awareness was the nature of the desire that motivated the ESP. If the desire is based on the setting aside of self in order to help someone in need, the necessary circle of Oneness is present and psychic awareness can be realized. If the real desire is to prove the existence of ESP, or to prove that a particular individual possesses psychic ability, then the wholeness of life is no longer the focus. Too often, the focus of skepticism is upon the existence itself of ESP. Instead, Cayce would have the skepticism oriented toward the helpfulness of a particular ESP experience in furthering harmony in life. In trance readings for a parapsychologist at Columbia University, Cayce advised that experiments should be focused not on "hits" and "successful subjects," but on the usefulness of the results. Cayce predicted that in the process of such a style of experimentation, we would learn all we need to know about the nature of psychic awareness.

## THE "DREAM HELPER CEREMONY": AN EXPERIMENT IN TRANSCENDENT PSI

Several years ago, I accepted the challenge to design an experiment that would meet Cayce's specifications for an experiment in transcendent psi. Meditating upon the ideal pattern involved in such an approach to research, I incubated this dream:

"We are gathered together for research and enlightenment. We are standing in the dark, not knowing how
to proceed. Suddenly, we begin dancing together in a
circle, each of us displaying an individual symbol. As we
greet and celebrate one another in turn, we realize we
have found our method, because the dance itself gener-
ates a central fountain of sparks to light our way."

The pattern of activity in this dream corresponds to
the pattern in a number of ceremonies and festivities
related to individuals in community. The May Pole rites
and the Native American Sun Dance ceremony involve
distinctively identified individuals dancing about a central focus. I enlisted the help of Robert Van de Castle,
of the University of Virginia Medical School, who had
studied ESP in traditional cultures and had participated
in some of the Maimonides dream telepathy experiments discussed earlier. Together we designed a group
dream-telepathy experiment: the "dream helper ceremony."

A group of people, willing to use their telepathic
dream power to help someone, are gathered together in
the evening. Within that group someone who is sincerely willing to ask the group for help with a genuine
problem of immediate concern volunteers to be the
"target person" for the group's dreams. The nature of
the problem is not revealed that night. Instead, the target person leads the group in a silent meditation prior
to bedtime. Upon retiring, the target person secretly
writes out on a piece of paper the problem for which the
group's help is sought. No instructions are given to the
group of "helpers," other than to remind them that
their dreams that night are not their own to forget, so
they must recall and record all the details. Here we have
a group of individual dreamers focusing their personal
dream processes onto a central subject, corresponding
to the pattern of the ancient rites.

If you can imagine being in such a dream helper
group, you can appreciate how it might feel preparing
for bed on such an occasion. You don't know what the
person's problem is, but you are certainly curious and
are trying to feel it out. You want to be helpful, but you

just can't believe it would be possible for you to produce a psychic dream. These factors create a strong sense of "unfinished business" at bedtime, leaving it to your dreams to resolve the matter through some form of connection with the target person.

The next morning the dreamers gather after breakfast, anxious to see what is in the collection of dreams. When asked, very few people think they have had dreams related to the target person. Not until all the dreams have been told, and their common elements noted, do people begin to suspect that their dreams contain something meaningful for the target person.

In one group several recurrent themes were apparent. The most vivid images dealt with *striking:* repeatedly hitting someone over the head with a hammer until they were dead; a boxing match, with two young men stiff-arming each other; young accident victims of a car crash; a guide drawing a group's attention to a brick at a Roman ruin that is dripping blood; and "a gory scene" from a film, "The Young Ones," about animals in the jungle. There were other animal images: rats running out of a cage; finding snakes in the back yard; and ducklings in about a foot of water—many dead. Another theme involved mother-child relationships: mother arriving at a movie theater with a young boy and an argument developing; a mother "in one of her most superficial moods and out of touch with her real feelings and not in touch with how the other person thinks or feels because of her usual self-absorption and self-centeredness" (the dreamer felt lonely, rejected or unloved by this mother). Another theme involved the concept of mental imbalance: stepping backward and nearly losing balance; "nuts" being cracked; being in a mental hospital. A final theme involved dirtiness and disarray: garbage day, and there are a few full cans; and "cleaning up the mess."

The target person, whom we'll call Patricia, was rather startled to hear these dreams from her helpers. Her question had concerned insecurities about making a career move. Hearing the dreams, she realized that her past was haunting her and undermining her efforts.

She volunteered to share some personal information about the "garbage" accumulated during her childhood. Her mother had suffered from significant psychiatric problems and Patricia perceived her as rather distant and aloof. Patricia often endured physical abuse from her, and on one occasion her mother had actually tried to kill her by placing her in a tub of hot water. The dream helper who had reported suddenly finding himself in a foot of water with many dead ducks and ducklings seemed to have tuned into this tragic event. It was possible for Patricia to relate to the idea of feeling like a "dead duck," or an "ugly duckling" because of the rejection she often experienced from her mother. She realized that the insecurities resulting from her childhood traumas affected her feelings about being acceptable in a new career.

In experiments involving multiple circles of dream helpers, distinct commonalities in the dreams of one group, as contrasted with another group, further suggest how the dreams are focused on something specific to each target person. Sometimes this type of difference can be critical to the healing potential of the ceremony. For example, I once was in a group dreaming for a woman whose problem concerned her repeated career failures. The dreams for her contained repeated references to aggression, assaults, forbidden sex, young girls, and daughters. The target person revealed suspicions of being sexually molested as a child. One of the group's dreams correctly envisioned the suspected circumstances of this event, in the cellar of the home. The central theme of the group's ensuing discussion had to do with how self-doubt and feelings of shame (in the target woman's case, related to the incidence of sexual abuse) contribute to blocks in creativity, an issue with which several people in the group were actively struggling.

By way of contrast, Bob Van de Castle was in a different group, dreaming for a woman whose question concerned the fate of her dead son. He had died under unusual circumstances and suspicions had been cast on a family member. Although no evidence was ever obtained, and the death was ruled accidental, the cloud of doubt had persisted for the two years since the event. None of the dreams for this woman contained any images of aggression, assault, or foul play. Instead, several dreams involved tripping and accidents, and many references to natural disasters. No sexual dreams were reported. The majority of the dreams contained references to sons (none to daughters), and to crying and grief, questionable evidence, fires to put out, and poor communications. This group concluded that the ruling of accidental death needed to be accepted so that the family could renew open communications and go on with its life.

When our two groups met to compare notes, Bob's target person was much impressed by the noticeable differences in the two sets of dreams. Whereas in my group there were many instances of aggression and foul play, not a single dream reflected that theme in Bob's group, where accidents and natural disasters predominated. That comparison helped the woman to accept the validity of her group's suggestion that her son died accidentally.

One way of telling if the dreams are helpful is in the long-range impact of the ceremony upon the target person. In Patricia's case, for example, a year later she was beginning a new career. She indicated that the ceremony had motivated her to seek therapy to rid herself of the emotional hangover resulting from her childhood rejections, and she was now in training for a new career. The woman whose child died under mysterious circumstances wrote a letter to Bob that said that she felt a great load had been lifted from her mind after the ceremony's conclusion. She had discussed the matter with her family for the first time since the boy's death two years before, and they were now on the road to recovery from this tragedy. Such feedback tends to support the validity of the type of help that comes from the ceremony.

The dream helper ceremony has been conducted by others with similarly beneficial results. It is interesting to note that most dreamers believe that their dreams are not on target when they first recall them, before the group meets to discuss the dreams. The ceremony shows how often telepathic information can be hidden in a dream. Only by comparing dreams does the psi factor come to light.

Not all the ESP is hidden. Occasionally, a dreamer has an extraordinary dream involving lucidity, hearing voices, or some other factor related to transcendent dreaming. In one case, a person dreamed of flying over the target person and announced that the "diet" was to blame. Indeed, diet proved to be a crucial factor. I once dreamed that I was lying on the deck of a sinking ship. The water level was rising slowly, but was beginning to enter my mouth. I began to choke and woke up abruptly, with the inexplicable impression that the target had been ill and almost died. As it turned out, the target person had almost died during a recent stay in the hospital. As an unexpected side effect to some medication she had received, she developed a temporary partial paralysis in her sleep. As a result, while sleeping on her back, her saliva filled her throat, choking her, and she almost died from suffocation.

The target person can identify elements in most of the dreams that touch upon the person's life as well as upon the undisclosed problem area. It is especially fascinating to discover that if the dream helpers go through the process of analyzing their dreams in terms of their own life situations, further areas of correspondence are discovered between these personalized dream interpretations and the target person. In one of my dreams, for example, my personal library was sitting out on the lawn. The image meant nothing to the target person. When I revealed what prompted me to begin to collect books, however, and what lawns meant to me, the target person and I discovered that we shared a desire for self-directed, noninstitutionalized study. It was a motive that played an important role in that target person's dilemma. Invariably, the impression is that the helpers definitely "tuned in" with their dreams. What seems to be the focus of the tuning is what the target person's undisclosed problem evokes in the community of the dream helpers. To reveal this deeper level of psychic interaction, however, requires additional cooperation from the dream helpers. They must set aside the role of "helper" and be willing to expose their own personal issues that are expressed in the dreams. Doing so has the benefit of creating a healing circle for the entire group.

A group image and the target person appear in some of the dreams, reflecting the nature of the experiment and its aftermath. The group discussion takes on a definite therapeutic tone. Although the original intent of the dreaming was to help the target person, the emotional sharing reveals how the dreams are relevant both to the target person's critical situation and to unresolved aspects of the dreamers' own lives. Before going to sleep, each dream helper seems to engage his or her instinctive, projective empathy to intuit that aspect of the target person's undisclosed problem that naturally corresponds with an unreconciled issue within the dream helper's life. Then, having been reminded of that issue, the dream helper's dreams perform their usual work of reconciliation, using his or her own experiences as well as images telepathically received from the target person's life. In such a manner, the group's dreams collaborate on a common problem as perceived from individual perspectives.

Astonishment, delight, and awe often emerge as the group marvels at what it has accomplished through its combined dream talents. One helper likened a group's efforts to composing a group symphony that was made possible by splicing their dream tapes together. Helpers generally feel that they have been so effective because they were not attempting to gain something for themselves; they were engaged in a healing service nourished from a sense of love. But the helpers are surprised to discover how much they personally derive from the process—the helpers are helped too.

The ceremony gives a group an opportunity to function as a psychic consultant to help someone in distress. In one special study of a dream helper ceremony, described by Jean Campbell in *Dreams Beyond Dreaming,*

the dream helpers' dreams proved to be more helpful
and on target than a reading from a professional psychic
hired to participate in the research. The dreams also
proved superior to the efforts of a professional counselor, who was hired to uncover the historical background of the target person's presenting problem. The
target person was harboring a traumatic secret that the
counselor had no way of knowing about. The helpers'
dreams went right to it and revealed its relevance. The
target person was relieved to have the opportunity to
unburden this secret and was helped to learn of the
bearing it had on the current problem.

The ceremony provides a repeatable demonstration
of apparent psi dreaming, with many of the characteristics of spontaneous cases of ostensibly psychic dreams.
But does the dream helper ceremony really demonstrate dream telepathy? The distinct and focused set of
correspondences in the collection of the group's dreams
could certainly be scored as hits, apparently accurate
psychic perceptions. But are these correspondences
more than coincidental? Traditionally, scientific parapsychology would focus on a statistical answer to this
question. The number of "hits" in a collection of
dreams for a target person would be compared, for example, to the number of "hits" in a collection of dreams
that were actually unrelated to the target person. In
fact, positive, significant results have been obtained with
the dream helper ceremony in this manner.

In one experiment, conducted by Mark Thurston, 244
people were recruited through the mail to serve as remote dreamer helpers. Each helper submitted a dream
sample. Four months later, two target persons were recruited in the experimenter's locality and randomly assigned to the dream helpers. Each dream helper
received only the name of the target person and was
asked to try to dream something helpful for his person's
undisclosed problem. The resulting "helpful" dreams
and the sample dreams were typed on index cards, shuf-
fled, and given to the respective target person. The target persons were asked to decide for each dream
whether or not it contained any resemblance to the

question being asked ("direct hit") or to any aspect of the target person's life ("indirect hit"). An independent judge was also asked to perform the same task, looking for "direct hits" only. When the number of judged hits for the dreams of the experimental night were compared to the number of judged hits for the sample dreams, the "helpful" dreams were favored to a significant degree for one target person, whereas for the second target person, "helpful" dreams and control dreams were equally likely to be judged as "hits."

Thurston followed up the statistical analysis by determining if any of the "helpful" dreams were actually helpful to the target person, who was suffering from a skin ailment. On the morning of the interview with the target person, he dreamed of her, saw that her rash had healed, and asked her if she had noticed all the dreams that dealt with diet. Thurston told the target person this dream. Together they examined the "helpful" dreams and found fourteen about diet. She agreed to work with her diet, returned in another month, and her rash had cleared.

One effect of our participation in dream helper ceremonies is to question the limits we usually place on the interpretation of dreams. To discover that your "ordinary" dream actually contains meaningful images from another person's experiences makes you wonder just how personal your dream time actually is. Although our dreams nevertheless serve our own personal needs, we may be intertwined while we dream more often than we suspect. Robin Shohet, in *Dream Sharing,* reports that when dreams are shared routinely in a contained community, overlapping themes are constantly discovered. She quotes one community member, "I let myself be aware that the unconscious mind of many other, apparently disparate people, was probably composing my dreams as well as their own."

# DEVELOPMENT OF PSYCHIC ABILITY IN COMMUNITY

Besides demonstrating an approach to transcendent psi, the dream helper ceremony also illustrates another dimension of Cayce's philosophy of developing psychic awareness—the community, or group aspect. The first step Cayce gave for developing psychic awareness was learning to cooperate. He also believed that cooperating in a group that is working to develop psychic awareness is quite appropriate. In the dream helper ceremony, for example, no attention is given to "who" had a psychic dream. Instead, the group cooperated to bring about generalized psychic functioning within the group's awareness. In the context of a cooperating group, it is easier to adopt the transcendent viewpoint, "psychic awareness *is,*" and leave behind the self-focus of "who" is exhibiting the most ESP.

After all, psychic awareness is the result of our being interconnected. Its ultimate source is in our interrelatedness. Ira Progoff, concluding his dialogues with the entities channeled by Eileen Garrett, noted that at some points in their conversation the depth of contact between himself and the "entity" was so great that it was hard to determine where the source of the intelligence lay, except to say it was in their interaction. Further evidence that it was the quality of their interaction is the fact that nowhere else in Garrett's own writings are these "higher" entities mentioned. Their appearance seems to have resulted from Progoff's presence and intentions. Progroff wrote, "It is important to remember that when we reach out into the larger meaning of things we are all reaching together, primarily because we are not able to reach separately and alone. It is thus that the Oracle dynatype [Progoff's term for the universal intelligence] of Mrs. Garrett cannot express itself and cannot be a channel for Tahoteh and Ramah [the two higher "entities"] unless a receptive person is there to evoke the depths of her psyche and to draw this image of the oracle forth in its dramatic forms." His statement echoes Cayce's claim that the quality of the readings he gave were a function of the desire and level of attunement of the person seeking the reading.

When Cayce was asked to lay out a program for developing psychic ability, the body of study material and exercises that he outlined were presented for use in a group format. The two-volume text of the study material that was developed is titled *A Search for God*. The content of study (the spiritual, or transcendent concepts of "Cooperation," "Know Thyself," "Love," "Opportunity," "Ideals," "Patience," "Happiness," and "Meditation," to name a few of the lessons in the text) is only one part of his approach—the part that is attended to the most. Many of those concepts have been presented in this book. The second part, the style of study, is equally important, but more often overlooked. This material needs to be worked with in a *group*. The group format has become known as a *study group*.

A group of people make a commitment to help one another and be supportive in learning the concepts related to psychic awareness and spirituality. Part of learning the transcendent orientation is discovering that we have more in common than we have differences. In the dream helper ceremony, for example, people often find that their dreams point not only to the target person's problem, but to how that problem is related to their own lives. The sharing in a study group raises the level of trust and caring among its members. As they begin to cooperate at deeper levels, psychic connections between members begin to appear. Ask anyone who has been in a study group for a long period of time and you will hear plenty of stories of psychic events. You will also hear stories of joint endeavors, mutual aid, and such that are reminiscent of the community spirit that we associate with an earlier era in history. The life and history of the group begins to undo much of the separation and alienation that industrialized life has generated. As a result, psychic awareness begins to thrive in the group. Psychic awareness is an attribute of a community of people who recognize their interdependence and sensitively act accordingly. Psychic awareness is not really intended as a power tool for the "loner" who wishes to step out ahead of the pack. Psychic awareness is not an expression of an isolated ego, but of the recognition of connectedness.

# PSYCHIC AWARENESS: HARBINGER OF GLOBAL CHANGES

Edgar Cayce is often associated with the prophecies he gave concerning coming earth changes. Like Nostradamus, Cayce foretold earthquakes, wars, and other upheavals. Less well known is that he predicted that a major dimension of upheaval would occur on the inside, within our consciousness. As the vibrational patterns in the fourth dimension undergo transformation, the effect will be experienced psychically by everyone on the planet. In *Visions and Prophecies for a New Age,* Mark Thurston interprets Cayce's prophecies of internal strife as the psychological reaction to a "paradigm shift," a change in how we perceive reality.

A major element of this shift in worldview is already evident. It is the transition to a holistic perspective. In the area of psychical awareness, it is a shift away from the term ESP in favor of psi or transpersonal, suggesting an order of reality above the single individual. Like Carl Jung's image of the archetype, Cayce's formulation of the creative patterns of vibration is being increasingly incorporated into modern thinking. People are becoming more sensitive to dimensions of consciousness that transcend the individual mind. We are witnessing the erosion of an artificial barrier that has maintained the illusion that our minds were separate. Psychic awareness is beginning to permeate human consciousness—and, as it does, there are upheavals.

It is as though a flood were rising in the mind. As the waters rush in, dissolving the walls between us, together we are cast upon the waters. Will the waters wash us away, or will we swim in them to a new life? Cayce suggests that the answer depends upon our preparedness. As psychic awareness becomes more of an influence in consciousness, those that have practiced "becoming psychic" will find the waters familiar. Part of that development is to extend one's identity to include a holistic vision of all of creation. It involves a near-death experience of our atomistic self-concept and a birth of a transcendent vision of self.

The earth as a whole has been subject to some near-death experiences, visions of the end of the old and the coming of the new. Jung interpreted UFO sightings and Marian visions as collective visions, representing an eruption of the archetypal unconscious into the mind of the masses. He saw these events as harbingers of significant changes in our consciousness. In *The Final Choice,* Michael Grosso argues that UFO sightings and visions of Mary are planetary near-death experiences. By his use of the term he means to suggest that all the attributes of a near-death experience at an individual level are applicable to these global visions. Such experiences come at moments of crisis, when physical life is threatened to an ultimate degree. That threat is upon our planet. An individual who has had a near-death experience identifies less with the body and more with consciousness. On a global level, it would mean our collective realization of the consciousness that unites us, the transpersonal level of consciousness.

Such a realization may be what lay behind the international celebration in August 1987 of the *harmonic convergence.* This term, coined by José Argüelles in *The Mayan Factor,* is the name he gave for an influx of new patterns of creative energies that were predicted by the millennial Mayan calendar. In light of our earlier discussion of such terminology, it is of interest that he chose words reflecting the imagery of psychic imagination, and that he suggested that we "resonate" to invisible "patterns" that would be "in the air." It is also of interest to note the tremendous response to this image—even though, judging by most news accounts and the explanations of harmonic convergence given by its enthusiasts, his complex book was barely understood, if read at all. But its image spoke to the imagination of the people, an imagination that is becoming more in attunement to the psychic.

Cayce, however, would add, as did some ministers in their letters to the editor about harmonic convergence, that attuning the imagination to the psychic is only part of the process of getting ready for the New Age. None of us will be able to maintain the peace of mind, nor the integration of the chakras, necessary for consistent and constructive psychic awareness until the stresses in the lives of other people are ameliorated. The development of psychic awareness in humanity at large will increasingly require us to take positive, concrete steps to apply the truth of the Golden Rule, to become our brothers' and our sisters' keepers. We must learn to cooperate. Psychic awareness is an expression of love, a love that needs to be as real in the application as in the imagination. In the application comes the awareness: that is Cayce's secret to awakening your psychic powers.

# SELECTED BIBLIOGRAPHY

Blair, Lawrence. *Rhythms of Vision: The Changing Patterns of Belief.* New York: Schocken Books, 1975.

Bolduc, Henry Leo. *The Journey Within: Past Life Regression and Channeling.* Virginia Beach, VA: Inner Vision, 1988.

———. *Self-Hypnosis: Creating Your Own Destiny.* Virginia Beach, VA: A.R.E. Press, 1985.

Bolen, Jean Shinoda. *The Tao of Psychology: Synchronicity and the Self.* San Francisco: Harper & Row, 1979.

Bro, Harmon. *Edgar Cayce on Religion and Psychic Experience.* New York: Warner Books, 1970.

Delaney, Gayle. *Living Your Dreams.* San Francisco: Harper & Row, 1979.

Garrett, Eileen. *Many Voices: The Autobiography of a Medium.* New York: Putnam, 1968.

Goldberg, Philip. *The Intuitive Edge.* Los Angeles: Tarcher, 1983.

Hudson, Thomas Jay. *The Law of Psychic Phenomena.* New York: Samuel Weiser, 1968.

Irion, J. Everett. *Interpreting the Revelation with Edgar Cayce.* Virginia Beach, VA: A.R.E. Press, 1982.

———. *Vibrations.* Virginia Beach, VA: A.R.E. Press, 1979.

Kautz, William H., and Melanie Branon. *Channeling: The Intuitive Connection.* San Francisco: Harper & Row, 1987.

LeShan, Lawrence. *The Medium, the Mystic and the Physicist: Toward a General Theory of the Paranormal.* New York: Viking Press, 1974.

———. *From Newton to ESP: Parapsychology and the Challenge of Modern Science.* Wellingborough, Northamptonshire, England: Turnstone Press, 1984.

Pike, Cynthia. *The Miracle of Suggestion: The Story of Jennifer.* Virginia Beach, VA: Inner Vision, 1988.

Puryear, Herbert B., and Mark Thurston. *Meditation and the Mind of Man,* rev. ed. Virginia Beach, VA: A.R.E. Press, 1978.

Reed, Henry. *The Dream Quest Workbook.* Virginia Beach, VA: Inner Vision, 1987.

———. *Getting Help from Your Dreams.* New York: Ballantine Books, 1986.

Sparrow, Lynn Elwell. *Reincarnation: Claiming Your Past, Creating Your Future.* San Francisco: Harper & Row, 1988.

Stanford, Ray. *The Spirit unto the Churches: An Understanding of Man's Existence in the Body Through Knowledge of the Seven Glandular Centers.* Virginia Beach, VA: Inner Vision, 1987.

Sugrue, Thomas. *There Is a River.* Virginia Beach, VA: A.R.E. Press, 1973.

Targ, Russell, and Keith Harary. *The Mind Race: Understanding and Using Psychic Abilities.* New York: Villard Books, 1984.

Thurston, Mark. *Dreams: Tonight's Answers for Tomorrow's Questions.* San Francisco: Harper & Row, 1988.

———. *The Inner Power of Silence: A Universal Way of Meditation.* Virginia Beach, VA: Inner Vision, 1986.

Ullman, Montague, Stanley Krippner, and Alan Vaughn. *Dream Telepathy.* New York: Macmillan, 1973.

Van Auken, John. *Born Again . . . and Again.* Virginia Beach, VA: Inner Vision, 1984.

Van de Castle, Robert. *Our Dreaming Mind: History and Psychology.* Virginia Beach, VA: Inner Vision, 1988.

# INDEX

# ABOUT THE AUTHOR

Henry Reed, Ph.D., is a research psychologist with a private practice in counseling in Virginia Beach, Virginia. He is also the editor of a newsletter and a magazine column on psychic research for the Association for Research and Enlightenment and is a faculty member at Atlantic University.

Before moving to Virginia Beach in 1976, Dr. Reed was a research consultant to the C. G. Jung Sleep and Dream Laboratory in Zurich, Switzerland, and an assistant professor of psychology at Princeton University. At Princeton, he taught courses on Jungian psychology and dreams and offered the first regular course for credit in the United States on humanistic psychology.

His publications include numerous articles and two previous books: *The Dream Quest Workbook* and *Getting Help from Your Dreams*.

## THE WORK OF CAYCE CONTINUES

In the more than 50 years since Cayce's death, the organization he founded in 1931 has continued his efforts in helping people to understand the purpose of life, the role of psychic awareness, and other mysteries of the mind. You can get free information about the Association for Research and Enlightenment (A.R.E.) in Virginia Beach, Virginia by calling its headquarters: 1–800–333–4499.

The A.R.E. sponsors conferences and lectures throughout the U.S. and Canada on many aspects of Cayce's work—the potentials of the mind, how to use intuition and dreams in daily life decision-making, the mind-body-spirit connection in healing, in addition to many other topics addressed in the Cayce material. A considerable portion of the Cayce readings deal with a holistic perspective of health and the healing process.

The A.R.E. Headquarters—where visitors are always welcome—includes one of the finest specialized libraries to be found anywhere in the world. Its 60,000 volume collection includes hundreds of titles related to developing psychic ability, dream psychology, intuition, reincarnation, destiny and free will, the purpose of life, and the universal laws that shape our lives.

For those who choose to become a member of the A.R.E.—joining a worldwide network of tens of thousands—additional resources are also available. The organization maintains a list of health-care professionals who are interested in applying the Cayce approach. Members can borrow detailed collections of what Cayce had to say about specific medical and non-medical subjects—more than 400 different collections have been compiled and are available. You'll find fascinating subjects and life-changing ideas on a wide range of themes: psychic awareness, prophecy, reincarnation, meditation, spirituality, vocational guidance, ESP, intuition, and dozens more. Members also receive a magazine, *Venture Inward*, which includes columnists and feature articles on how to transform one's own life using spiritual principles.

The A.R.E. offers study groups in most cities, many local regional activities, an international tours program, a retreat-type camp for children and adults, and A.R.E. contacts around the world. The Cayce materials also form an integral part of Atlantic University (also in Virginia Beach, Virginia) which offers a master's degree in Transpersonal Studies, with options to specialize in several areas such as intuitive studies, holistic health, and the visual arts.

For free information about any or all of these programs, call the toll-free number listed above or write: A.R.E., Department M, 67th and Atlantic Ave., Box 595, Virginia Beach, VA 23451–0595.